I0762030

Odyssey

poems, articles, speeches, leadership study...

By Meredith Coleman McGee

Join the conversation on our blog www.meredithetc.com
The author's blog page: http://meredithetc.com/odyssey/

A Meredith Etc Book
1052 Maria Court
Jackson, Mississippi 39204-5151
www.meredithetc.com

Second edition 6" x 9" hardback
Printed by IngramSpark
Black & White on White - Pages - **260**
ISBN-13: 978-0-9993226-3-5

Second edition 6" x 9" Trade paperback edition
Barnes & Noble Press
Black & White on White - Pages - **260**
ISBN-13: 978-1-9870024-6-1

Foreword by Angela Stewart
Introduction by Mrs. Alma Fisher
Prelude by Ms. Willa Coleman Ridgeway
Special Poem by Miss Calla Ridgeway

LOC Call No. 2013496363

First edition 6" x 9" soft cover
Black & White on White paper - **228**
ISBN-13: 978-1491229118
ISBN-29: 149122911X

Key words: Poetry, U.S Economy, James H. Meredith, Southern History, Business Leadership, Meredith Coleman McGee

Cover: Meredith Coleman McGee, Posing in Las Vegas, NM

DEDICATION

Everett Herman Meredith, 1936 to 2018

PRAISE FOR ODYSSEY

The prose and poetry in Odyssey are both deep and thought provoking as each one tells a different story that speaks of the human struggle. The 'civil rights' history on James Meredith and others reflects the ***odyssey*** of a southern journey; we can all profit from the small business interviews and lessons.

Barbara Meredith Hardy, *Family Matriarch*, Michigan

Meredith Coleman McGee writes honestly about pain, human frailty, and difficult social issues, yet her poems reflect a tenacious, sometimes surprising, hope in the possibility of transformation, healing, and wholeness. As she both celebrates and laments our rich, but often troubled, collective and individual heritages, she reminds us that our journeys continue, and our striving for better things must never cease.

Alexis Spencer-Byers, http://alexisspencerbyers.wordpress.com/
Author, *Urban Verses*, Coauthor, *Stepping out From the Shadows*

Meredith's verse is a strong and edgy look at the everyday issues of life--from family ties to political lies--helping us see ourselves more clearly through her lens. Is it any wonder? Her uncle is famed Civil Rights icon James Meredith.

Jeanetta Britt, Award-winning author www.jbrittbooks.com

"ODYSSEY" is a fascinating journey in the layered mind of Meredith McGee. It's more than just a collection of poems, antidotes and recollections, but an elixir for the soul. She delves into the pain, hardships, and triumphs of our families and their "neighbors," giving mother-wit as well as scholarship for solutions. Nearly 300 pages of historical pictures, accounts and anecdotes, this book is a must read for aspiring minds! Great job cousin!

Ahmed Majeed, Descendant of the Patterson lineage.

TABLE OF CONTENTS

Odyssey

Join the conversation on our blog www.meredithetc.com
Author's blog pages: http://meredithetc.com/odyssey/
https://meredithetc.com/meredith-coleman-mcgee/

Foreword

The word odyssey refers to a journey or a trip. An odyssey can be either a literal or figurative journey. It is always a writer's goal to take his or her readers on a journey. This book is the 2nd edition of Odyssey which is a collection of Meredith Coleman McGee's writings from 1994 to 2018. The book includes poems, speeches, articles and a leadership study comparing the leadership styles of Ray Kroc (McDonald's), Sam Walton (WALMART), and Dave Thomas (Wendy's) with 12 business leaders from the southern United States.

I have known Meredith Coleman McGee for over 10 years; our mothers are long-time friends. Meredith Coleman McGee is a writer, publisher, acquisition editor and community activist promoting literacy and writing in her community. Meredith is the embodiment of the Kwanzaa principles, *Kujichagulia*, self-determination and *Kuumba,* creativity. She defines herself and as a publisher she helps others define, defend and develop themselves. Her activism is all about leaving her community better than she found it. She is committed to not only being a creative force herself but also helps others harness their creative energies. She is an active member and supporter of our book club, SANKOFA Reading Group.

ODYSSEY is inspired in part by her rich family legacy bestowed to her by her maternal great-grandmother, Roxie Hickman Patterson, her maternal uncle, James Meredith (the first African American to attend the University of Mississippi) and her mother, Hazel Meredith Coleman Hall.

ODYSSEY's poetry is based on family experiences, personal pain and African American history. The reader learns about trials and accomplishments of Meredith Coleman McGee's extended family, her ancestors, her parents, her sister, her nieces, and historical figures such as Congressman John Roy Lynch.

In addition to poetry, ODYSSEY contains speeches and articles written by Meredith Coleman McGee. The speeches and articles reflect Meredith Coleman McGee's community activism. Her commitment to promoting literacy is reflected in her campaign to form a group to support the Richard Wright Public Library in Jackson, Mississippi. Most of her articles were originally published in the Jackson Advocate newspaper.

ODYSSEY introduces the reader to a writer, activist, poet, publisher, and family member who is changing her community and making it better. The second edition of ODYSSEY expands on the work of the original volume. The reader will be changed and inspired by this book.

by Angela D. Stewart, Founder/President
SANKOFA Reading Group

PRELUDE O D Y S S E Y *by Willa Coleman Ridgeway*

O of Odyssey

Oddly enough we are offended often by those closest to us.
It's obvious that we become obstinate to these opinions.
The road occasionally seems longer than our hearts can bear.
So we become ordered and obstinate against all odds.
Operating on an objective philosophy; it opens our mind to more options.
Yet, we limit ourselves to our own oaths.

D of ODyssey

Dare to dive in the journey which delivers your soul satisfaction.
Did your dubious nature dump a load of devastating news on you?
Do you plan to drop your dear love off once it no longer benefits you, my dear?
Doing what develops one into a better person, determines deeper growth.
One does the deeds necessary to deem a better place.
Do you because it is definite?

Y of OdYssey

Why look at life from your perspective only if you live on an island does this work?
You are among others whether you depend on them or not.
You are full of your own perspective why not fill up on your neighbors whys and why nots?
You can yell or yawn from lack of interest but you still may need to say yes, I will listen.
Why do you feel it is better off missing, yet, young in your wisdom?

Yea to yahoo, cause without your yearning for others approval you would be just that.

S of OdySsey
Save me so I can see me clearly.
I am shaped to be solid but my existence seems shaky.
Set me free of such sanity allow me to seek what has sprang me.
Spoil me for sport because I am spread too thin.
Speak to what I am afraid to say.
Save me so I can see me sincerely.
Willa Coleman Ridgeway

S of OdysSey
Say! What did you say?
Sensual sexy some-things seep across my audible zone.
Say it again; didn't quite get what you said.
Take me on a journey saying what you said to me.
It seems so sexy that you say such things.
So say it again and again so my soul can sink in.
You said that something so I want to hear you say what you said, please say it softly.
So, I can hear smoothly, sense it, blow it.
So I can feel the breeze.
Just say something sensible sensually.
So I can hear you say something.

E of OdyssEy
Each person has a light evolving from dim to bright.
Everyone has an erotic place they envelop for special entry.
The enticed enter at their own-risk.
Explain with your eyes, who am I to you?
Ease into a new existence where you include each other.
An eyeful of energy passing by you and them cross paths.

Let your light erupt bright lasers through this evolution of erotic vision.

Y of OdysseY

Yep, I said it to you.
Yep, I said it about you.
Yep, I am coming at you like that.
You heard me right.
Yes, you see me stand in your space.
You step away emotionally I approach you more mentally.
You leave mentally I step closer to leaving.
Yep, I can yell but I shouldn’t care that much.
You really don’t deserve that heightened level of emotion.
You offended? Yeah right?
Willa Coleman Ridgeway

Short and simple

Short and simple
We awakened on our daily journey.
I walk to see passers-by.
Short and simple
I speak; you speak but why did we do that?
What really was gained other than simple courtesy?
Short and brief, we keep it simple.
Like a comforting slow breeze, gently across your face.
A short and sweet kiss across your full cheek.
Short and simple
The moments that life brings us, simply.

Willa Coleman Ridgeway

A long way

A long way to go, it's a long way away.
So, we begin. We start our journey.
Tired and shoes worn, it appears that I have a long way to go.
Speechless from being out spoken, I got to keep going.
Searching from not knowing I am still aware.
I got a long way to go, oh boy!
While we continue tell me what you know.
It is better planned or not.
Does spontaneity make it lighter or free you more?
Your long road is ending only when your last breath is leaving.
Long ago becomes your past and a long way to go is still lending.
We go forward on our journey as the words lay a trail for all that's pending, and what was representing your life's journey.
Willa Coleman Ridgeway

Just don't

Don't stunt my growth; don't stop it up.
Don't make me pump my brakes.
Accelerate my speed, let me get where I need to be.
Don't put my hope on freeze.
I got somewhere to be.
Don't hold me back.
Don't break my momentum.
Let me enjoy full speed until I no longer need to go forward,
And I find where I need to be.
Just don't hinder me, don't take away from what is good for me.
Don't tell me what's not meant for me, just don't.

Willa Coleman Ridgeway, AKA, Reya Peach, Poet/Lyricist, *Status Move* (CD)

To Grandma Hazel

You're such a great grandma to me.
I'm so confident knowing that,
I have someone like you by my side when I need you.
Thanks for being there.
Calla Ridgeway, Illustrator, *Saving the Manatees*
(children's book)

Calla Ridgeway (front left) Rashida Redmond (front right)
Ridgeway receiving "5th Grade Class Valedictorian Award"

Her relatives who were valedictorians (or equivalent) previously

Name	**Relation to Calla**	**Grade**	**Year**
Miriam Meredith	Great Aunt	12th	1944
Hazel Meredith	Grandmother	12th	1957
Joseph H. Meredith	2nd Cousin	PhD	2002
William E. McGee III	1st Cousin (step)	3rd	2002

Note: Miriam and Hazel were class valedictorians at Attala County Training School in Kosciusko, Mississippi. William was an honoree at Wilkins Elementary School in Jackson, Mississippi. Joseph (son of Civil Rights icon James Meredith) was named the Outstanding Graduate Student in the School of Business Administration at the University of Mississippi (Ole Miss) in 2002.

INTRODUCTION

Mississippi author Meredith Coleman McGee presents the reader with a triple expression of literary form in ODYSSEY, a uniquely written, well researched work which produces a family of fiction and nonfiction writings under one cover.

This book is an interesting read especially for the poetic minded, the Civil Rights activists, students of history, and small business leaders.

Of special notation is the prelude written entirely in a poetic fashion by the author's sister and niece. This one volume contains 228 pages with black and white pictures, charts and references.

The first three chapters consist of poems that mirror the behavior and conditions that are often seen in today's world. These human conditions exist in one's engaging journey for self-identification. Some of the poems are based on factual events; in one poem the author includes the experience of her ancestor in a four-line stanza.

Chapter four consists of pre-published articles by the author which respond to current and historically charged issues which provide valuable resources for a bevy of audiences. The articles include statistical and timely information about numerous topics and record facts about McGee's uncle Civil Rights Icon James Meredith's 2009 Walk for the Poor and his & 2012 Walk for Education & Truth.

In the final chapter, McGee shares the findings of her research project which was submitted to Antioch University McGregor, now known as Antioch University Midwest, Yellow Springs, Ohio, in partial fulfillment of her Master of Arts Degree. This study compared the leadership characteristics of Sam Walton and Ray Croc with southern small business leaders. Walton and Croc turned

Walmart and McDonald's respectively into global conglomerates. This study is heralding for leaders interesting in mirroring the leadership styles of successful entrepreneurs.

Alma M. Fisher, Tougaloo College
Retired Librarian and Archivist

SOMETHING CHRONICLED

Deceptive dreams

She had nothing but her dreams to cling to.
They had lied to her a thousand times.
They told her she lived on a hill in a white fenced house.
They said there were no cracks in the walls of her shack.
They said her lover was cheating.
They told her she slapped her supervisor with a dead fish at the staff meeting.
They told her she was the president of the bank.
They told her she wasn't a $7.50 an hour employee.
They said she could float in the air above the sea for miles.
They told her she wasn't his mark.
They said her mother fell in love with her trick.
They told her locust and honey were kosher.
They told her she had lived 2,000 years ago.
They told her she had danced with warriors.
They told her she slit a snake in two by the Bayou.
They told her she helped free 1000s of Africans in captivity.
They said her master was her daddy, and her cousin was her brother.
They told her she had been a master of slaves.
They told her she married her husband's servant.
They told her she defiled the purity of her race.
They told her she used voodoo for sport.
They said her dad was French and her mom was African.
They said her dad bought everything in the house,
but never dwelled in it.
They said her mama ran away.

They said her daddy hunted her mama down.
They said her mama fled to Canada and never returned. They said her daddy gambled away his fortune.
They said her daddy died broke as broke as can be.
They told her a fat cat stole her royalties.
They said her granddaddy was red as red as can be.
They said her Native American ancestors built mounds larger than the great pyramids of Egypt.
They told her a turkey egg could feed three or four.
They said her mama had a heart attack when she walked through the Door of No Return and never boarded the ship. They said her aunt jumped off the ship and never made it to the West Indies.
They said her uncle hid in the woods and lived among the Natives.
They told her granny stuck a pitch fork in Mister's hand.
They told her the sheriff buried Bubba's face in the sand.
They told her justice wasn't no woman with equal scales.
They told her jail was hell and wasn't no peace in it.
They told her the warden was a hypocrite, and the governor was his friend.
They told her tricky business practices will push millions into the pits of poverty.
They told her 12 percent of the nation was already broke and it wasn't a joke.
They told her to jump in the pond, but she woke up in the nick of time.

By Meredith Coleman McGee

Verses 18-20 are based on McGee's paternal great, great-grandmother, Adaline Adams (1843-1911), who was the widow of a slaveholder. In 1870 she married her servant, Parris Adams. He was 14 years her senior. His birthplace was South Carolina. Seventeen children were born to their union in Ballplay, Alabama which was where the Cherokees used to play ball. Though, she was white, Adaline was classified as black in the 1900 census, and 13 of their children were alive. Adaline is a common name of German origin.

What of life if liberty is a joke?

What of life if liberty is a joke?
What of life if liberty choke your throat?
What of life if money talks and poverty cries?
What of life if the city institutes a Black tax, endorses White privilege, and perpetuates poverty?
What of life if economic development can't touch lives now?
What of life if city fines, wages into obscurity?
What of life if hope is long gone?
What of life if a little girl is left at home alone?
What of life if a little boy is taught to hate his father?
What of life if a little boy's father calls his mother ugly names?
What of life if a mother tells her children their father is a bloodsucker?
What of life if a child can't determine if his hateful parent is a hero or a foe?
What of life if emptiness steals peace?
What of life if rotten punches the nose when the sun rises?
What of life if no one cares except the hungry dog?
What of life if weeds are taller than the flowers?
What of life if brute strength allows one to enslave another?
What of life if a crime scene is a regular childhood memory?
What of life is doping stole the cherry?
What of life is drunkenness is a daily state of mind?
What of life if one always picks a fight he/she can't win?
What of life if watching your back floods your mental space?
What of life if you and your neighbors spend all your money in another hood?
What of life if there is no one who believes you could?
What of 'this nation' if we could praise the leader who freed Pine Lawn?
What of the future if our government embraced innovation?
Why is a patent so high?
Why is there so much despair?
Why is an unarmed misdemeanor suspect required to lie face down on the ground?

Did city leaders prove they cared?
Why are the fines for the uninsured so punitive?
Why does a vehicle depreciate so fast?
What of the future if the preacher kept the teens in his/her mist?
What of the future if the teacher could impart common wit?
What of the future if the housewife could make a profit off her apple pie?
What of the future if apprenticeship was valued?
What of the future if respect was instilled from birth?
What if the 'happy song' flooded the air wave?
What of the future if parents didn't curse before their children got on the bus?
What of the future if love sat at the kitchen table?
What of the future if love was the law?
What of the future if Harriet wasn't history?
What of the future if Frederick could motivate?
What of the future if love replaced pain?
What of the future if the Spirit could teach the congressman to love?
What of the future if the man at the podium cared about others?
What of the future if love was stamped on the dollar bill?
What of 'the nation' if love could give liberty balance?
What of the future if classism was no more?
What of the future if moral consciousness could teach judges fairness?
What of the future if donors made sure every child had a book?
What of the future if the prosecutor could endorse fairness?
What of the future if 'the system' could teach the public defender to defend?
What of the future if the 'American Dream' was real?
What of the future if the government dared to care?
The End!

By Meredith Coleman McGee

An imprisoned mind

From the walls of prison, I cried for my unborn child and my cellie[i] ignored me.

From the walls of prison, I felt pity for my sins and those committed against me and my cellie laughed at me.

From the walls of prison, I gained knowledge of my heritage.

Ain't' that something! If my grandmother was a Choctaw Indian, where is the pottery in our family loot?

Why are her people oppressed on a reservation?

Why am I in prison?

Why didn't my English grandfather leave some of the gold or the little house behind the mansion?

Why did my grandfather peep at my mother through the window and never touch her pretty face?

Where is my African father's castle - his royal estate?

Why am I penniless? From the walls of prison, I became free and my cellie adored me – the daughter of nobility.

So, I bought some Indian pottery for our family loot, earned me some dust and built a mansion, and I rode an elephant's back across my father's estate.

From the walls of freedom, I became rich and my cellie partnered with me – the Nubian queen – the seed of confusion – the black child from the east.

Verse 8 is based on a story about the author's maternal great, grandmother, Roxie Hickman Patterson (1874-1947). According to family lore when Roxie, a Mulatto, was a little girl her English father Harvey Davis, a powerful County Judge requested for her to be brought in front of his law office so he could peep at her through his window. The incident was humiliating. Plus, Judge Harvey had abused his power over his teenager servant, Roxie's mother, Arteal and impregnated her at age 12. There were no legal protections for Black women in those days. Therefore, the damage of sexual assault and social humiliation was colossal. Information about Roxie and family history are included in the biography *James Meredith: Warrior in the America that created him*. James H. Meredith also discusses family lore in his memoir, *A Mission from God: A Memoir and Challenge for America.* Roxie H. Patterson was his maternal grandmother.

Grandma MeMe

TRIBUTE TO:

Beulah Mae Adkins Coleman Sealey Thomas
1921-2017 (95.5) years old

By Meredith Sealey Coleman McGee
Bobby Joe's oldest daughter

Beulah was her name.
Family was her claim to fame.
She held Robert Coleman (Bobby Joe) in her bosom.
John Sealey Jr. came one Summer.
Bobby Joe was a mean linebacker.
Big M he was called.
John was Little M.

Meme was five generations strong.
She was a Voter Registration Educator for SCLC.
She marched with Martin Luther King.
She learned civil disobedience at the Freedom School.
She hosted Andrew Young and Civil Rights workers.
She led the first sit-in in Gadsden with the Girl's Youth Choir.
She was jailed for 11 days.

Beulah was her name.
Styling was her thang'.
She was too cute to be called grandma.
Her grands settled for Meme.
Class she had plenty.
Bridge kept her going.
She was an Alabama girl.
She was a Buffalo Bill's fan.
Went to church on Sunday.
Once owned a red convertible and a white Cadillac.
Paid tithes faithfully.

Loved Cracker Barrel, good company, and delicious food.
Adored boss wags, nice jewels, and laughter.
Loved God and her fellow man.

Beulah was her name.
Heaven is her home!
Her spirit lives on!
Love!

McGee wrote this tribute for her paternal grandmother's funeral program. Beulah Thomas passed June 26, 2017 at Buffalo General Hospital, Buffalo, NY and was buried July 3, 2017 next to her nephew James Herring in a cemetery plot near the late Music Legend Rick James.

The blame game is the enemy

She had no one whom she could truly trust.
Too many cling to hate like a venom.
Few admit their own mistakes,
placing blame on others – on anyone.
Blame it on mama. Blame it on daddy.
Blame it on the ex. Blame it on the ex's spouse.
Blame it on the supervisor.
Blame it on someone else's dysfunction.
Wait! Look in the mirror!
Wasn't it you who couldn't get along with your co- workers?
Haven't you had twenty jobs in the past decade?
Wasn't it you who walked away from your job?
Wasn't it you who walked away from your blood?
Yes! You walked away and left the child you brought into this world sitting in the high chair at your mother's house with a nasty face.
Yes! You! No one else! Your mama raised him. You didn't. Stop giving her hell!
Stop encouraging him to hate the woman who raised him. The woman who made the sacrifice.
The woman who paid his bills.
The woman who paved his way.
The woman who taught him how to rake the yard. The woman who taught him gardening.
The woman who sent him to summer camp.
The woman who took your boy on vacations. Did you? The woman who held him when he cried over you.
The woman who listened to him vent over you.
The woman who taught him forgiveness.
The woman who was true.

The woman who gave birth to you, too. The woman who bore it all, while you roamed the streets with the beast. Stop giving your mama hell girl!

Starry and rural leaders in Rural America

Starry is her name. Infinite is the seed she planted.
Rural leadership is her claim to fame.
Development is her passion. Network is her trail.
Stories flowed in the room like the big river.
The circle of sharing spread to the edge of the earth.
The rainbow of life echoed throughout the day.
The little girl sang merrily, and happily away.
The soul on the mound met the man in the valley.
Miss Sally made a pie, Carol shared her herbs.
Knowledge is golden, common sense is free.
The visitor slept in the tepee and not in the loft.
Injustice across the nation was tattered and told.
At the end of the meeting a senator rose, a business owner sold, a nurse healed,
A teacher taught, a mother fought, a father fended,
Starry reigned and the network - Never Ended.
To the future of a pretty world changed one policy at time.
Can you spare a dime or teach mouths to grow food on a vine.
No debtor's prison, no disrespectful minors,
no abuse from authority.
Let love, decency, honor, humility, and peace in the mist.
Miss Sally made home-made soap, and Ben picked potatoes.
A rainbow of people sat at the circle of sharing and shared and still do.
The spinning wheel is spinning and rolling from coast to coast,
From north to south, from Belize to Mexico, and from South Africa to China.
Miss Sally made home-made bread, and oppression flew over the coup.

By Meredith Coleman McGee

Imitation of Life

Black boy, black boy, don't you see, the world is waiting for you to be who you'll be.
The hurdles ahead are many, but success is hard to find.
Hurry, hurry to the bar the first 50 will get in free.
Your future girl may be there or maybe a one-night stand.
The package lurks near, on the wall, hot potatoes.
O dear, O dear!
The line outside is long, so the show will be prolonged. Keep your eyes open, don't dare doze for long because your enemy is everywhere.
Bad spirits and confusion can turn friends into foes, because good dialogue is hard to maintain.
It must be one way or the other because compromise is always at stake.
Keep a clear head often, calm will see you through, but erratic behavior can destroy you.
Your little brother is watching and waiting to grow fast. He wants to be just like you because you're the man he sees.
He loves his mother dearly, but she abandoned him too soon.
She left last Sunday after dinner and returned to retrieve her things.
His eyes rained tears for hours, and nothing has mattered since.
He yearns badly for his mother, but she is lost to boot. Toot, toot around she has been, but worries she has none because fun is sitting at the door when her eyes meet the sun.
The boy grew up too bitter to see the glitter glow, while little brother portrays the imitation he knows.

Hold your head to the sky

Hold your head up toward the sky.
Don't cry. Don't get mad.
Your mind will flip, and your words will trip.
Don't worry, don't fret, better days are ahead.
Don't dread, don't cry, you'll make it somehow.
The burden is heavy and times are hard.
Plan ahead.
He laid his head on a concrete bed.
All of his earthly belongings were in the grocery cart.
He lives under the bridge near Highway 14.
His wife passed above often on her way to work.
His son is a sheriff and his daughter is a teacher.
His wife prays for him every night.
She works at the car plant assembling car parts.
He was stuck in a rut and didn't want to be found.
His bed is still on the ground.
His name is not Harry, but it is simply – Zack I don't care.
He is not a fictional character, but real and not a lie.
His family cries for him, but he appreciates the scraps.
He hasn't earned a cent since he parked his Cadillac.

The empty mistress

Moments after the mistress discreetly embraced her lover, she walked into the club alone.
Her hair was light red and styled in a fluffy sequence.
Her large looped earrings and her manner of dress made her appear younger than her years.
Her life was full of fears.
Her outfit was piercing pink, trimmed in lace, and revealed her left shoulder.
Her marriage had grown cold.
Her husband was home fascinated with his gin and tonic, his friends, and laughter.
She and her lover hung out at the club uninterrupted twice a month.
Her lover's wife entered the club to attend her sister's birthday party.
The mistress was startled when the wife entered.
The mistress followed the wife through the club.
The mistress greeted the party guests & surveyed the area.
The mistress sat at the bar behind the party participants.
She waited patiently to test her lover's loyalty.
By midnight she had danced twice, but her lover had not shown his face.
The wife ate and mingled with the party guests.
Her husband was afraid to show his face in the place.
He feared hurting the feelings of his wife and his mistress.
He hurt them both just the same.
He told them both over their cell phones he was on his way, but he didn't join them.
He received a call around 10 pm detailing the seating positions of his wife and mistress.

When his wife went home he hugged her tight and rolled off a good lie.
When she fell asleep, he called his mistress and they laughed for hours on the phone.
He found comfort knowing his wife and his mistress were in different locales.
The mistress passed by her husband who was in a deep sleep on the recliner.
Their love had died a slow death.
First, he lost his job. Then, he refused to look for work. Then, he fell in love with gin and tonic.
Then, he fell by the wayside.
Then, he lost his drive to strive.
Then, he lost his fervor for life. Then, he became childlike, sitting at the table waiting for someone to put food on it.
The mistress cried for hours.
In her home, she had a boy in a man's body.
She had another woman's man in her head.
The boy in the man's body left her responsible for the bills.
Her double life rendered her a villain.
The boy in the man's body was himself ostracized.
The boy in the man's body left her empty.
The boy in the man's body left her alone.
The mistress and her lover were cheaters.
Steal away - oh my!

Freedom and Liberty

The blood of Nada spilled in the street of Iran and stained her "Where is my vote? SIGN" which was laying in the street.
Her rallying cry was heard across the globe, but her government silenced her to speak no more.
Her family tore their clothes and wept and wept.
They remembered their friend who was stoned in the street.
Give me liberty or give me death Patrick Henry cried back in 1775.
Not much has changed. History repeats again and again.
Must you deny the people their rights?
Does it have to be this way?
People continue to use your voice to improve this world.
You can't stop now, this we know FOR SURE.
Keep singing and walking in the streets - if you will.
Till freedom, liberty, and equality cover the globe, and the voices of the people are heard here and there and everywhere.
Democracy, Democracy where were you when they killed Jimmie Lee Jackson and beat mama to sleep?
Democracy unless you deliver freedom and liberty, the cloak of death will knock this world to its knees.

The legacy

Her father left them hanging and took his money with him.
His rejection hurt them deeply; they hung their heads low.
The boy had no daddy to walk him through the park.
He wouldn't sweep the driveway or wash his mother's car.
He was lazy and predicted to be nothing.
The Christmas tree was tucked away in the dark.
Their socks were thin and the air in their rooms was mist.
Their clothes were worn and giving.
The girl rejected smarty pants and fell in love with a bicycle thief.
Smarty pants was elected to school government and stood out from the rest.
The bicycle thief became a petty hustler and the girl followed suit.
They crept bubble gum from the corner store, marked it up, and sold it at the park after dark.
He eventually took a lashing and moved to Tanszulu.
The girl loved a con artist. He sold fake dreams for cash and threw her love in the trash.
Along came a player who left her at the altar,
and his crazy ex threw red punch on her wedding gown.
Her distorted face lay motionless in a zigged frown.
Upon her stumbled mister one evening at the mall.
She clung to him for peace and kissed him on the cheek.
She used her hustling skills on something legit.
They build a retail business and hired 100s of clerks.
They were honored by the Chamber and featured in the news, but OH HOW that money gave them the BLUES. They lectured at seminars & travelled around the world. The boy grew up, raised another man's children, and boy he loved them so.
He read to them every night and walked them to school.
He told them every day never be anybody's fool.
He gave the girls away and hung their wedding portraits high.

He became known as simply 'grandpa' to a new generation.
His love was deeper than blood for that was all they knew.
He deeded his heart to his family.
He made a lie out of his past, and was honored by his daughters.
They hung his portrait high.
Their neighbors heard them singing sweet words to him looking above toward the heavenly sky, "*Papa was a good man, don't you know, he taught us everything we know. Papa was a good man, don't you know, he brought us up right and we thank him so*."

The odds of losing

The man squeezed that dollar so tight, goodwill went out of sight.
He knocked his workers to their knees, and cut their throats with pennies.
They filled the cracks in the shanties with paper, but they shivered senselessly because the cold was there to stay.
The odds were against the salesman.
The percentage was rigged to starve.
How can you fill your belly when life is too hard?
Nelly climbed the charts, Michael and Janet screamed, but poor Nancy's meal ticket ruined when her lights were disconnected.
No pie at home for Eddie cause' Carol packed her bags, and cleaned their bank account and took all that he had.
So sad, so sad, was he, but his spirit moved alone, and soon Eddie's pocket grew big and strong.
It takes one to know one, but not in every case, for throwing things in his face will only give her a headache.
He clashed with philosophy, but no one knew just why.
Billy Bob lied on the witness stand and found 5 alibis.
He went away for nothing and boy was time inside hard, outside was faintly better, but all together vain.
What pain must one bear to walk along the shore?
Find the money door when you're ready and vain will reign no more.

Go away dysfunction

The man screamed when he disagreed with anyone.
The man's son screamed when he had a different point. The man's grandson screamed when he debated the issues. The men in that family had the tendency to scream.

The woman obsessively loved her baby more than any of her children.
The woman's daughter obsessively loved her baby.
The woman's granddaughter obsessively loved her daughter more than she loved her son.
These women had a hard time balancing their relationships with their children.

The woman drank until she passed out.
The woman's daughter smoked herself to sleep.
The woman's granddaughter was sober, but she read obsessively.
Some obsessive behavior is fruitful.

The insecure father ignored his daughter until she was 23.
The father's daughter ignored her son until he turned 18. The man's grandson ignored the loving foster parents who raised him.
A disloyal fruit replenishes the unhealthy pain bestowed upon it by the giver to a victim.

The man slept with the woman.
The man slept with the woman's sister.
Their sin tore their families apart.

Journey of influence

History precedes life's journeys.
The past is the stem of one's path.
Every individual takes his or her place in this life.
Some grab life by the throat, and shoves spirit and righteousness in this world, and shakes things up, and moves mountains.
Stories of these movers awaken generations and influences the future.
The world holds many stories.
Be implored to learn the great ones.

Prelude poem for the biography *James Meredith: Warrior and the America that created him* by Meredith Coleman McGee

Lynch Street

Years ago they say, "The Jackson City Council approved an ordinance to name J.R. Lynch Street in honor of John Roy Lynch."

Well, this is a story about John Roy Lynch.

John was the son of a wealthy planter, Patrick Lynch and his slave Catherine.

John was born and raised in Concordia Parish, Louisiana, in the flatlands off the Mississippi river near Natchez.

When Patrick died, his arrangement to free his half white and half black son and his mistress were not allowed, so the boy and his mother became the property of another slaveholder.

Even though educating a slave was forbidden by law, the new owner saw to it that John learned basic reading and writing. Later, Catherine and her son John were sold to a slave holder in Natchez, Mississippi.

A change gotta' come!

In 1864, John was freed from slavery by the Union Army. He began to read a lot and he attended night school to further his education.

In 1870 Negro men obtained the right to vote (15th Amendment U.S. Constitution).

By 1872, John had learned Mississippi Jurisprudence and was admitted to the bar as an Attorney in Natchez.

A change gotta' come!

John joined the party (Republican) of Abraham Lincoln.

When the opportunity came, John was elected Justice of the Peace of Adams County.

In 1869, Lynch was appointed to the first Mississippi Negro College Board.

In 1871, Mr. Lynch campaigned and was elected to the Mississippi House of Representatives.
At age 25, he became the Speaker of the House.
Money was raised and in 1872, Alcorn Agricultural College opened its doors to Negroes.
Later that year, Lynch, a former slave and a self-educated man was elected to the U.S. House of Representatives. Lynch was elected three times and served Mississippians in his Washington, DC office.
A shoe string district was drawn which diluted black voting strength and Lynch lost his re-election bid.

Then, President Rutherford Hayes, a Republican, made a deal with the Democrats.

After less than a dozen years, the Negroes' political power was forfeited, he became disenfranchised, and Jim Crow was born. White women obtained the right to vote in 1920, but the Negro had to wait almost 90 years to obtain widespread voting rights again.

Malcolm X said, "The Ballot is more important than the dollar." Men like Lynch, when elected, negotiated bills which became laws that benefited America's dark children.
If political power is as mighty as the dollar bill, what are we doing with our ballots?

Lynch Street is named for a great man - John Roy Lynch.

Raise them up! Power to the People! Power to the People!

The lethal game of chance

He implored his crew to play a simple game of Russian Roulette.
One of them protested, but he was called a coward.
“Look at him, he’s scared. If you scared call the Po Po?” In total agreement the crew agreed to play the lethal game of chance.
A single round was placed in the revolver.
The leader spun the cylinder and snapped it in place.
The teens played the dozens and laughed over their fear.
The first player (the leader) placed the muzzle against his skull and pulled the trigger.
The odds of the gun firing on player one was 16%.
The gun did not fire on player one.
The second player placed the muzzle against his skull and pulled the trigger.
The odds of the gun firing on player two was 20%.
The gun did not fire on player two.
The third player placed the muzzle against his skull and pulled the trigger.
The odds of the gun firing on player three was 25%.
The gun did not fire on player three, four, or five.
The sixth player placed the muzzle against his skull and pulled the trigger.
The odds of the gun firing on player six was 100%.
The gun fired on player six.
He immediately fell to the left of his chair.
His blood spilled on the floor.
The ambulance classified player six DOA.
The players wept.
They had not known the risk involved.
Three of them were only sixteen.
They had seen the game played in a movie.
They had been impressed with the actors.

They had assumed the game would prove their bravery.
They had not known the game would steal one of their lives.
Russian Roulette is a deadly game of chance.
There is nothing brave about playing this deadly game.

The lethal game of chance was written in memory of teens in the Virden Addition community in North Jackson who lost their lives in the early 1990s to the deadly game of Russian roulette. These teens were patrons of Sunrise Foods # II on Mayes Street.

James Meredith's lounge theme poem

Stick around at James Meredith's Lounge.

Where poet's 21+ speak words of fun and clown, every Friday and Saturday night from 8 to 10 pm.

Where BYOB and a jukebox sings 3 for $1 and 8 for $2. Where the 8 ball falls and a player wins.

Where the atmosphere is high, and mess will end, cause too much gin ain't' our friend.

Must be 25+ to lounge late – bring a date.

Where the voices chatter every Friday & Saturday from 8-2 at 217 West Griffith Street near the rebirth of King Edward, where the train stops twice on a pretty night in the Farish Street Historic District.

This poem was written in August of 2009. At that time, Meredith C. McGee and her husband Will were overseeing the operations of James Meredith's Lounge for a brief period. The building is now the site of Jackson Taxi which Second Reconstruction education pioneer James Meredith owns and his daughter Jessica manages.

The stranger's spring

Where were you last night, when the rain pounded against my
window and the loneliness sunk in?
Did you know I was here?

With no one to love me, no one to hold me, no one to talk to,
cause' you were gone and I alone!

Where are you now? While the sun shines so pretty and the
flowers bloom. And I feel like spring inside – so warm – so
needed.

I hear a knock on the door – this isn't you – what must I do?
The stranger enters and he sits and he sits and he sits and I
become comfortable.

The stranger sits and he sits and he holds me.
The stranger sits and he sits and he loves me and I love him back.
I feel like spring inside – so warm – so fulfilled.

The stranger is good. Goodbye my love, the stranger is here!

Published: Howard Ely, Timeless Voices, Owings Mills, MD: The International Library of Poetry. 2006. This poem was written by Meredith Coleman on March 18, 1998.

SOMETHING INSPIRING

Mirror on the wall

Why is the blue sky gray?
Will his soul reach heaven on judgment day?
Is he prepared to lead? Please, Please, Please!
Have u any manners to speak of?
Did his voice reach the man?
What is your five-year plan?
Will you save, will you spend, will u make amends?
Mend a broken heart, a shattered life, a strained relationship.
Mend a broken fence, blend your mind, touch a heart, play cards.
Who are u? Are u blue?
Are u going anywhere?
Are u daring, glaring, bold or brave?
Is your dream on a mountain in the sky?
Are u winning the game of life or asleep and in defeat?
Are u a man or a boy, a woman or a girl?
Are u the ruler in your house, or a mouse, or a bug? Sneaking through the night gathering bread crumbs.
Are u a bum?
No, He's fly. He's it. He's spit.
Want some? Some what? Yup. What is Yup?
Yup is what it is.
Mirror on the wall, are u balling, shot calling?
What u gonna' do when they come for you?
Are u blue, are u true? Who are u?

Let your light shine

Let your light shine, like the rising sun.
Like the dawn of fall, like a falling star.
Like the light from the moon at night when they're holding hands, and playing footsy in the sand.
Let your light shine like the glitter of gold.
Like the dawn of morning.
Like at night when she feeds him a spoon full of pecan pie.
When you push her away but your eyes tell her to stay.
The thrill is on is a song.
But the thrill is real when the night is still.
When the wind shakes the leaves on the trees, and the mind is set to please.
When sweet melodies play a tune, and love is planted on your mind, and your face appears in her eyes.
Let your light shine, so you can fly to the top of the skyline, pass the clouds toward the heaven up above, like a dove with white wings, bringing peace to the world.
Let your light shine lover; let's sail to Cancun; let's sail real soon.

Weeping mom

Mama, mama don't you weep.
Your shoes are cheap, but your values are pure.
Your hair is nappy, but your mind is strong.

Hold on, hold on, stand your ground.
Look life in the face pound for pound.
Her child joined her hater's club,
and threw her love in the mud.

She didn't allow his hate to place her mothering in the vain lane.
She turned that bad energy into a force,
and played the rising game.

Rise high, rise high, and don't you lean.
Show all the haters they can't win.
Their hate will never doom you in.
Mama, don't slow down.
Someday you'll earn your royal crown.
Someday your feet will paint the town.
Someday a smile will replace your frown.

O' ungrateful one with the pea brain, what goes around will come back to you.
If your snobbish ways don't end, your days will linger.
You spit on the hand that fed and clothed you, and cursed the leadership that led you.
You honored those that threw you away, and kicked those that held you up.

Mixed up and confused, you missed your learning curve.
No fool can learn with deaf ears.
Arrogant one, you forgot to remember.
What a plain shame.

The shining angels from Heaven

The shining angels are the angels from Jesus.
The shining angels from Heaven kept us and watched over us all the time.
The shining angels never left us.
The shining angels always loved us and took care of us.
The shining angels always kept their rings around us.
The shining angels are the ones that Jesus sent to us all.

By Darlene D. Collier
Published in the memoir *Married to Sin* © 2013

Little Susie Q

She walked off the school bus into his Cadillac.
She had a Mac attack; so he treated her with a snack.
She vented to him for hours.
Her pain was piercing deep, for she had lost both of her brothers in a brawl at the corner store.
He listened attentively, but their outings ended quickly cause' granny pulled the rope.

Fascinated with her; he studied her like a book.
He interviewed her friends and former classmates.
He asked her for her cherry, but she refused repeatedly.
He showered her with pretty things,
but granny sent them back.

His passion for her grew with every teasing moment, and he fretted something awful after every 'no.'
Her big eyes mesmerized him.
Her smile drove him wild.
He listened to her for years and waited impatiently.
On her high school graduation day, he gave her a card.
When she finished college, granny invited him for supper.

On their wedding night he cried like a boy, for his virgin wife was enough for him to continue to adore!

Rebuilding

The walls screamed at the woman.
The doors slammed in her face.
The floors cracked. The ceiling split. The burden grew.
The doors screamed at the woman.

The house was consumed with hatred.
A fungus ate away spots in the grass.
The squirrels ate the peach seeds. The tree began to bleed.
The ugliness brought her to her knees.

The floor screamed at the woman.
The walls, doors, and floors lost their compassion for her.
The river overflowed; the house flooded.
The woman abandoned the house.
The walls cried. The doors became lonely.
The floors mildewed. The ceiling sunk.

The woman built a new home.
The grass was pretty and green, and she picked and ate the peaches.
The walls listened, the doors celebrated her, the floors comforted her, and the ceiling loved her.

Smile Child

Smile awhile child.

It's not as bad as it seems.
Go ahead and scream. Not too LOUD, PLEASE.
Scream silently inside have some pride.
Say a prayer if you dare.
Think peaceful thoughts.
Dream peaceful dreams.
Rise above it all.
Pick the paper off the floor in the hall.
Give a helping hand.
We know u can.
We believe in u.
You're the glue to your future.
Make it happen, get snappy.
Clap to the beat, stomp your feet.
Feel the rhythm of the drum.
Plant your dreams on the sun.
Kick the crap to the moon.
Dismiss the sad-song-be-gone.

Smile awhile child.

It's not as bad as it seems.

Life lessons

The woman and her son toted two buckets of water to her old Chevy truck from their neighbors outside faucet to pour in their toilet so they could flush it.

The toilet worked but two city workers dressed in blue uniforms removed their water meter because it was connected illegally.

A woman with the Lord's Prayer taped to her cubicle said the illegal connection fee was $100.
The mother tried to borrow the money to pay the penalty and the past due balance.

She asked her son's father if he could help but he refused, even though he hadn't paid child support in six years.
He offered to allow his son to spend the weekend with him, but he refused to give her any money.
The boy spent the weekend with his father, but returned that Sunday evening at 7 to a house without water.
A week later the mother pulled up at the water company in her old truck and paid the fine & fee.
Their truck was loud and the paint was worn and faded.
The boy wished he and his mother had a nice car.

Three years later the father pulled up in a new luxury car.
He took his son for a ride every now and then.
The boy was happy to take joy rides with his father in his nice car.
The mother and her son's days of toting water ended.
She remarried and moved into a new home.

That summer the boy's father was imprisoned because he owed $40,000 in back child support.
The boy rode with his uncle to see his father the first visiting Sunday. His father embraced the boy.
As they exited the prison gate, the boy cried, "If daddy wasn't here, he could be taking me for a ride today."

The secret revealed

The son grew and he grew and he became a teenager.
The son grew and he grew and he became criminally inclined.
His adventures in crime landed him a 10-year sentence.
He did his time. It was hard. Stuff happened. It happened.
As he was riding the bus up Highway 49 toward home, he straightened his posture in his seat.
He thought wildly how to keep his secret concealed.
His family embraced him when he descended the bus.
He had only seen his mother 3 times in the last decade;
he hadn't seen his father at all.
His younger brother lifted one of his taped boxes and put it in the trunk of the car.

Other than attending church, he lurked inside the house endlessly afraid to meet the tiger.
He thought he could avoid the beast, if he stayed hidden.
He declined invitations for yardwork, paint work, or any work.
The hours turned into days, the days turned into weeks, and the weeks turned into months.

And on the 1st day of the 4th month, he secretly ventured outside in the wee hours of the morning.
The outings went from sporadic to nightly.
One morning he barely missed his father in the kitchen retrieving a slice of apple custard.

He slowed down the outings a bit for fear of discovery.
But on the following Wednesday he ventured out again.
He returned but forgot to take off his club clothes.
When the clock passed five a.m. he met his mother in the kitchen.
He was startled and he stood there speechless.
His mother spoke softly, "You forgot to take off your lipstick."

Beaten mind, body, and soul

On stage she was a rock star,
at home she was degraded.

At work she was the director,
at home she was defamed.

At work she was the principle of the school,
at home she was abused.

At home she was a wife,
who was constantly faced with contention.

The screaming made her nervous.
The name calling spun her mind.

The screaming sunk her spirit to the ground,
and buried her soul in the road.

No peace was at home for her,
only soiled relationships.

She pondered over her tears how to improve her situation.

She didn't pack her bags,
but she walked away that day,
and never returned.

She has harmony at home these days.
She doesn't live in fear, and
she wakes every morning to uplifting words of cheer.

She dreamed before she woke

She dreamed she would write a poem.

She dreamed she would escape her miserable existence.

She dreamed the sun would shine on her pocket, and fill her purse with large bills, that she would awake and find the bills paid, her bank account in the clear, her stock holdings rising, her life tamed, and her love not in vain.

She dreamed she could write a book, day by day, and in due time, chapter by chapter.

She dreamed their votes would count, their lives would matter, their children would have a bright future, that the schools would be filled with learning, that the children would press for success, desire to learn their history, and never repeat the poor mystery.

That good teachers would earn equal pay and want to stay.

That boys would learn from their fathers to love their mothers, respect their playmates, and to adore their dates.

That their girls would want to be like role models, who covered their bodies, and held their heads high.

She dreamed that youth would love their ma mas, appease their pa pas, adore their elders, listen to positive people, and beg for wisdom.

She dreamed they woke up and realized there is much to change.

That their children shouldn't be bad statistics.
That the jails shouldn't be filled with their young men and boys.

That some of the toys should be books, should bring knowledge, so children can get a trade, learn a skill, or go to college.

She dreamed before she woke, that they cannot go on this way, that it does not hurt to be serious, that it does not hurt to read, that they are destined to succeed, but they must give up some of their jive because they were born to rise!

The grass is green sometimes

The grass is green where love reigns,
where blood flows through the veins,
where preachers teach the truth,
where children blossom,
where gloom is doomed,
where despair is rare,
where mama cooks wholesome meals,
where a deal is fair,
where granny is the nanny, and the children learn at home, what to do, how to do it, and what not to do,
where the house is clean, and daddy ain't mean,
and mama is loving because she feels like a queen,
and the children play fair
because they are aware that bullying,
can get cut up and brought down fast,
because constant teasing won't last,
won't last, cause' sooner or later,
the victim might tear up that ….

The family connection

Money makes the world go round and round it goes,
high in the sky like a flock of birds,
like a bird building a nest for her birdies to grow.
She pushed the birdies out you know and made them fly, but they didn't die.
Like a bird chasing warm weather, cause cool ain't' in.
Calm is better; wisdom is desired.
Think before you speak.
Your words are cutting; they're too much to take!
You're raw – get it together.
Too much stormy weather - Heather
It's not that serious – don't you know,
believe it - conceive it.
It's there in your reach – get it while you can!
Hold your mouth once in a while, speak uplifting words.
Make announcements cautiously.
Don't expose the private parts. No one should see.
Keep it in; hold that sin.
Be strong, live long, love long, and bring peace!

Unite the family.

Don't you dare bring them down to your ground.

Your ground is hard – it's cold – that mess is old.
They forgave you – forgive them.
Grow up, look around – what do you see?
Do you see the woman that made you be?
the man that bears it all… the brother that rigged the lights.
Yes – for you too. No doubt. It's true get with them.
They love you.

Can't you see – your family – sit down – be cool.

Sit! Okay!

A message to sisters

There is a message in music.
There is a message in songs.
There is a message in lyrics.
There is a message in poems.

One day the lyrics of Bobby Womack spoke to her soul, and a light went off in her head when he said, “You won’t always be sweet 16 while you are carrying a little weight find someone who will mean you some good.”

There is a message in music.
There is a message in songs.
There is a message in lyrics.

And sisters Bobby brought the message home.
Bobby said he was an entertainer and like most entertainers and men, he would be here today and gone tomorrow.

Most men will hit it and quit it.
Most men will be with you today and gone tomorrow.
But a good man will be with you when the sun goes down.
A good man will stick around when you’re down.

They say, “A good man is unique and quite different from the rest.”

They say, “A good man will give you his best.”

There is a message in music.
There is a message in songs.

While you are carrying a little weight, find a decent mate and build a happy home.

SOMETHING BLUE

Where was peace?

Where was peace man when brother was sitting on the corner, almost in tears, smoking a Marlboro, wondering why his dad hadn't called in years, and why his mother could barely pay the bills?

Where was peace when the little girl was staring out the window because she didn't comprehend the day's lesson plan, hadn't done her homework, and was sad because she heard her parents screaming all night which kept her poor mind uptight?

Heartaches and pain cause daily strains, and make good folks wonder, how to keep from going under, how to make everything okay, how to roll with the punches.

But, throw a few punches with the speed of Ali, or with the power of Iron Mike.

Keep throwing punches as you travel through life, and if you knock down enough barriers, you will ride down Highway 5, light as a kite flying the clear skies, guided by a little boy with his father on the beach.

Keep going and going as you will, and the rain will turn into sunshine, and grief will cease and prosperity will linger until the light of dawn on the foot of the moon, but you must knock down some barriers, enough barriers soon.

Then, peace will clear your mind and give you rest, and give you rest and give you peace.

The unwatered plant

He slapped a frown on her crown.

The plant was not watered and it withered and died.

She forgave over and over again.

Her chin became attached to the palm of her right hand.

The season changed; it rained and it rained and the plant fell from its frame.

He pushed her here, hither, and there.

She left her faith sitting in the chair.

The reason for the season blew away like the mist at night in the dark alone in the park.

She stood tall, she held on tight, and fought her feeling through the night.

The owl peeped through the tree making his presence known.

That morning she pondered, worried, fretted, and cried.

The chicken jumped over the fence.

Dinner was served without meat.

He shined his shoes, told her he was sorry for the 12th time, and headed east.

By noon, confusion had taken a toll on her soul.

She snapped the string beans in 100 pieces.

The sun jumped over the moon, but the message arrived that afternoon.

She threatened to harm herself.

Her sister told her, "Go ahead."

Words sis would one day dread.

She cried for help; they went to her side.

She cried for help; they went to her side.

She cried for help; they screamed wolf.

She cried for help; they yelled wolf.

She gave up the ghost.

They dressed in black, and rode in that pretty Cadillac.

She is no more.

They all cried at her graveside.

Fakology

Flee from me u poisonous snake.

U are a phony and a fake always out to take.

U carry a smile of shame - as if you're carrying FAME.

U dodge responsibility because your soul is empty.

U pimp the innocent with your lies of love and deceit.

U wear that big smile in vain, but u ought to be ashamed.

Your kind of love does God awful things.

U teach your children fakology.
U poison their mind with your devil wine.
U put a bone on their plates AND crumbs in their bowls.
U missed the school play, the game, and the tears.
U showed up when your daughter signed her record deal.

But you didn't show your face when she broke her heel.

Keep lying u poisonous snake.
God knows u a phony and a fake.
U fooled the world with that big smile and those lies.
But the Man in the sky knows the lie behind your eyes.

U won't get by on judgment day because the truth will bury the lies in your eyes, and strap your soul to the dungeon WALL with the HOGS.

U greedy pig!

Your FAKOLOGY will cease at the end of week.

Missing you

Grandma, Grandma where are you?
I song you a verse over the phone and you gave me a snort.
Baby girl held you hand and got no reaction.
Your present state dropped a bomb on hearts!
That homemade air didn't preserve your smile.
That homemade air isn't preserving your movement.
Grandma, Grandma where are you?
I miss the updates about your latest joke.
Daddy misses hearing your voice.
They say I should be happy, but I am blue.
The nurse can't tell, can't tell.
What's happening, please tell me.
I want to know before the angels let go.
We miss your voice. We miss you.
We whispered softy — no snort, not a motion.
Grandma, Grandma what is this?
Forgive me God, I know she is your child.
We miss her so.
Her wish is ignored with that homemade air.
God move the dictator!
Give her rest — give her peace.

By Meredith Coleman McGee
Summer 2017, June 20, 2017

McGee wrote this protest poem because her paternal grandmother's medical proxy ignored her grandmother's wishes by removing her from hospice at home with her granddaughter and great granddaughter and placing her in a cold hospital...

The Bookstore

She was holding her head in her hand, sitting in the chair - crying, staring at the wall, because her love was in the hospital remembering the incident at the bookstore in the mall.

When they were accused of stealing a money sack.

Thieves they are not.

His work clothes were dusty; this is true, but they were in the bookstore shopping, looking for books on the sales table, searching high and low.

They collected a stack of books and had money to match.

You treat consumers badly.

You had them thrown on the wall.

Their person was searched by the police; they were accused of stealing on Christmas Eve.

What a treat for last minute shoppers who fit your stereotypical view.

They were working people, though their skin is black.

They didn't take your money sack.

They earn an honest pay, but don't worry - don't you weep, they'll never patronize your bookstore again.

They'll always be black, but they're never coming back.

The Bookstore was based on a racial profiling event which happened to Meredith and her husband, Will, at Books-a-Million in Jackson, MS; while Christmas shopping on Christmas Eve (2005) for book gifts to give to family members, the couple was approached by a male Jackson Police Officer, who escorted them to an office in the rear of the building based on an employee's tip. The duo were questioned. Will had to remove his jumpsuit and was searched. It had splashes of mud on it because he and others had just completed a plumbing job. A female officer was called to the scene so she could search Meredith's person. When the officers discovered the employee's allegation was unwarranted, store management was chastised. The incident was an extremely degrading and crushing experience to the couple. Unfortunately, racial profiling is problematic for People of Color across the country.

The old ex-marine

The old ex-Marine lay dormant in his hospital bed with one inch finger nails, sore smelling feet, and bedsores from Nursing Home neglect.

He had become blind, could not walk, but he talked, grunted, and dreamed.

His water and juice glasses were full and his meal was untouched.

Chapped lips were a sign of thirst; a light snore and rigid sleep bore witness of chronic disease.

The queen he loved stood not at his bedside. His demise was hastened by grief; no Dorothy entered the scene, no wizard played any tricks.

His thoughts grew warm in remembrance of Maria, who once loved him before his hair grayed.

In the sky above, the love from his father – Old Black Joe – reached ground and relieved his pain, and touched his hand and he stopped longing for a life that had passed by, and a love that had withered and died.

He made amends for past sins; he longed for a son, who had preceded him in death, and for peace to give him rest.

He prayed a prayer and God held him tight, and took his soul from his earthy fight, with his eyes shut tight and his diabetic fingers folded and bent, where his red sore feet lay on freshly cleaned linen, changed by a hospital nurse who cared, and a human who shared.

An angel saluted the old Marine as he stood in limbo, waiting for his maker to straighten his fingers, allow him to stand on his two feet once again, to have people love him in spite of distant illusions, and countless excuses.

He longed for a soft touch to hear a song from his mother, and be embraced by his father.

He remembered Maria, who rendered him with pleasant memories of a time long gone.

She gave him hope for the future, but the doctor had to feed him fluids intravenously.

His nurse cut his fingernails, and nursed his wounds; he found peace, he healed, and then he became a chatter box.

"Don't give me no red beans, don't give me no rice, I ain't' gonna' tell you once, ain't' gonna' tell you twice."

Call, "See you later alligator."

Response, "After while crocodile."

"Hey, hey let's have some fun. Give me a honey bun."

The closed womb

God closed her womb too soon, which tore her heart apart.

She wanted just one wish which was to have a baby girl.

God closed her womb too soon.

She never felt her kick in her stomach.
She never heard her first word, or saw the first fall, while she was going up the hall.
3 years passed by; she discovered it was not meant to be.
She cried every day without tears,
and every night in her sleep.
Surgery could not solve her infertility,
and she learned to accept her fate and so did he.
She was what she was.

But if she could have given birth to a girl.
If God would have allowed a girl to enter their world, they would have named her 'NANDI.'
NANDI was an African queen in South Africa.
She was the mother of Shaka Zulu.

God closed her womb too soon.

If NANDI would have come.
They would have taught her African,
Indian, and World history.
They would have told her that
Shaka Zulu was one of the Great Kings of Africa.
That he changed South African warfare and conquered a territory larger than the continent of Europe.
That he took the throne that had been taken from him and his mother by his brother.

That he was driven to strive because he hated his father and loved his mother.

God closed her womb too soon.

If NANDI would have come they would have taught her to be driven to succeed from an inner peace that one gets from love.

God closed her womb too soon.

The other dreams will live;
no more, their dreams, won't die.
They'd pave a path, carve a whole,
and never again lose their souls.
The girl didn't come but they are still one.

God closed her womb too soon.

No more, their dreams, won't die.

Loud mouth trash talking man

Don't need no loud mouth trash talking man.
Don't need no man calling them dogs, hogs, hussy, or ucky.
Needs a good man going somewhere in life - a nice talking man.
They like men to call them boo, cutie pie, or...

Grandpa said, "You gets what you give."
Treat folks nice and they'll treat you nice.
Talk to people nice and they'll talk to you nice.

Stand by a woman and she'll wipe the sweat off your fevered face.

Bring you breakfast in bed - comb your nappy head.
Help you make a bright future; just treat her right.
Treat her right and everything will be dynamite.

Don't need no man don't take care of his babies.
Need a man that will make money and handle his business.

Don't need no loud mouth, trash, talking man.
Need a good man, going somewhere in life,
a nice talking man, a man with a plan.

SOMETHING SPOKEN

Chapter 4 *Something Spoken* contains speeches and a presentation which was presented by the author at Historic Greater Ebenezer Baptist Church, before the Hinds County Board of Supervisors, and during the Conference on the Status of Women 61.

Meredith Coleman McGee, *Speaker*
Historic Greater Ebenezer Baptist Church,
Bogalusa, Louisiana
Blogs: www.meredithetc.com – www.typingsolutions.biz
www.shopheirs.com – www.mosedpress.com
Facebook: https://www.facebook.com/meredith.mcgee.31
LinkedIn http://www.linkedin.com/pub/meredith-mcgee/4/a8b/76a
Twitter: meredithetc

Monday, January 16, 2017

Yesterday matters--The future must be planned

There is nothing nowhere on earth like southern hospitality. Thank you for your hospitality. Bogalusa, Louisiana.

It's an honor to be here today. I understand this church was used for large gathering during the Civil Right Movement.

The stories of old are lessons for today.

MLK Day is a national holiday because Martin Luther King Jr. was a great leader. He was bold. Bogalusa was bold.

Martin Luther King was born, 88 years ago, on January 15, 1929.

Be a part of the solution. Cecily Tyson said, "Take your place." Thank you for holding down the fort!

Rev. Dr. Louis Blake Hathorn's book ***Social Justice and Christianity*** described Martin Luther King as the most powerful Black leader that ever walked the earth in North America.

Martin Luther King and Ralph Abernathy founded the Southern Christian Leadership Conference, known by the acronym SCLC, in 1957. Sixty years later it is still producing drum majors for justice.

MLK Day.

My 95-year-old grandmother Beulah Sealey was a voter registration educator for SCLC. She taught people how to fill out voter registration forms. She led the first lunch counter sit-in in Gadsden, Alabama in 1965. She and a dozen teenage girls were jailed for 11 days. Martin Luther King and Andrew Young visited them in jail.

Remember the adage: ***the pen is mightier than the sword***. It is! Yes sir. Yes ma'am.

Martin Luther King's speeches were written and recorded. His thoughts were penned in books. Powerful stories inspire new generations to fight battles.

Martin Luther King and Ralph Abernathy launched an attack on evil forces during the middle of the 20th century. *Evil forces remain among us.

*Dylann Roof is an evil force. I am sure you've heard about him. He massacred 9 church goers at Emanuel African Methodist Episcopal Church. He was recently sentenced to death. He publicly admitted he has no regrets.

He said, "**I had to do it**!"

Martin Luther King, Ralph Abernathy, and others planned every march, every campaign, and every attack against evil. They listened to the voices of the community. Alabama citizens from other parts of the state drove to Montgomery and attended SCLC's meetings. My grandmother and others from North Alabama were sitting at the table.

Back then, people were working together for a common cause – justice, equality, dignity!

Freedom is life! Bondage is death!

On November 6, 1956 Martin Luther King wrote:

But if physical death is the price some must pay, then nothing could be more Christian

Like Christ!

Martin Luther King knew the risk involved in being a drum major for justice.

Martin Luther King was inspired by Mahatma Gandhi. Gandhi's words, speeches, and thoughts were written.

The pen in mightier than the sword!

You see, one day in another land (India) far away from America, Gandhi was leading a non-violent revolution. He told his countrymen:

Rivers of blood may have to flow before we gain our freedom, but it must be our blood.

Mahatma Gandhi was assassinated in 1948. Martin Luther King turned 19 that year. Gandhi's story was written. The written word is powerful. Martin Luther King read about this great Indian freedom fighter.

The biblical story of Moses inspired Nat Turner. **The Birth of a Nation** was a hard movie to view, but it revealed a lot about our ugly history.

Like Gandhi, Martin Luther King, Malcolm X, Medgar Evers and many others paid the ultimate price – death– for their race.

We must remember A.Z. Young, Robert Hicks, Gaye Jenkins, and many others.

Our grandparent's stories are very important.

My great grandmother Francis was born in 1865. Her daddy - JAP Campbell - had owned her mother during slavery. He educated Grandma Francis. She brought literacy to our family. My great grandfather Ned Meredith signed an X on his marriage licenses. He and his first wife and first set of boys were illiterate. Grandma Francis was Grandpa Ned's 2nd wife.

Mothers are usually a child's first teacher. The alphabets, basic math, and a child's first words should be taught at home beginning at age 3.

Every child must go to school prepared to meet the challenge. Today, anyone can buy books at Dollar Tree or take their children to the library.

I saw a news story this morning on Channel 9 about a 4-year-old girl who has read over 1,000 books. She has a large vocabulary. Reading comprehension goes a long way.

Don't let anybody fool you, it's cool to be smart. Smart people get the good jobs. High paying jobs. Most highly successful people read for pleasure.

Learn your family history too. Ask your grandparents about their childhood, their parents, and other experiences. Upload your family video to your YouTube page. Now, that is important to preserve.

During the middle of the 20th century, Black men in Bogalusa stood up and told their White employer at the paper mill, "unfair hiring and promotion practices" must change.

When the employers of the paper mill resisted, they were met with resistance.

These are old stories, but local history is very important to understand.

We must understand were we have been. Certainly, a politician should understand the history of laws.

People around here remember when Robert Hicks threw his shotgun over his shoulder to protect himself and his property.

Citizens remember other members of the **DEACONS FOR DEFENSE AND JUSTICE**.

The DEACONS FOR DEFENSE protected Civil Rights workers.

They protected my uncle James Meredith as he finished the last leg of the ***Meredith March Against Fear*** June 26, 1966 with Martin Luther King, Stokely Carmichael, James Farmer, and others.

James Farmer can here, back in the day, to help you. I came here from Jackson, Mississippi to speak to you. We are in this together. This is serious business!

Justice and the progress of our people!

The ***Meredith March Against Fear*** was the last massage march during the Civil Rights era.

The youngest nationally known leader's rallying cry of "Black Power" in Greenwood that Summer gave birth to a new era.

Stokely Carmichael recalled that Martin Luther King *never talked against other leaders. Carmichael said backbiting was not good for the struggle. He said he learned not to talk against leaders of organizations because organization is permanent.

SCLC is still here. The NAACP is still here. The Bogalusa Voters League is still here.

James Meredith was shot on the second day of his ***Walk Against Fear*** in Hernando, Mississippi by a white unemployed man from Memphis. He was the first white man to be sentenced to serve time in Parchman Prison for committing a violent act against a

Black man in our state. I believe he served 18 months. Today, James Meredith is 83 years old.

Fifty years ago, our skin color branded us a group, and united us by a common bond of brotherhood.

Today, drugs, gangs, and sometimes greed has divided us.

Chicago is full of division. Chaos is everywhere.

I read that some guards at Angola were recently busted for selling contraband to prisoners. They were fattening their pockets. The payphone companies are fattening their pocket. Angola Prison was once the Angola Plantation. Our state penitentiary Parchman Prison was once the Parchman Planation. *Hard labor, harsh realities, inhuman conditions.

Imprisonment is a form of slavery.

The love of money is the root of all evil. Last year, a Tennessee prisoner penned the evils of contraband smuggling in his novel ***Death by Association*** Vol 1 ***Retaliation*** Vol 2 ***Deception***. In his story, Green Dots are used like Swiss Bank Accounts.

Green Dots have done a lot of good for participants on the Steve Harvey show. The evil use of Green Dots is another story.

The Voters League is still here getting-out-the-vote, and being a voice for citizens.

Martin Luther King Jr. had a dream. Mahalia Jackson encouraged him to share his dream with the world that Summer day, August 28, 1963.

Rev. King dreamed that White America would respect our kind, give us the right to vote, give us a fair wage, treat us with dignity, and allow us the opportunity to live the 'American Dream.'

Yesterday matters--The future must be planned

You see, 50 years ago, a hung jury could have spared Dylann Roof.

You see, we still have work to do. The American Judicial System is flawed.

Money can pay for good lawyers. Good lawyers can work miracles.

Public Defenders often tell the innocent to plead guilty.

Guilty pleas can strip voting rights and can make one unemployable.

The future must be planned

Every child in this city should know what happened in Bogalusa in the 20th century.

The knowledge of self is the greatest knowledge for any people.

Our history in North America didn't begin with slave ships which were blessed by Popes.

African heads are not carved in stone in Mexico for nothing.

African sailors navigated to North America long before Columbus.

We don't need a national holiday to learn. All we got to do is open a book and read it.

Extra! Extra! read all about it. Study to show thyself approval!

Our history begins with the beginning of man. Not with Ham.

We were not cursed. No curse changed our skin black.

The oldest human remains were unearthed in Africa.

Egypt is not far from Ethiopia.

Yesterday Matters

Yesterday was Sunday, January 15, 2017. The birthday of MLK.

The future could be Friday when Pres. Barack Obama leaves office and stands to witness the transfer of power to Pres. Elect Donald Trump.

John Lewis is speaking his mind.

Maxine Waters' CSPAN comments were blocked out. America is divided.

Fifty years ago, one of our top priorities was the right to vote.

Today, our college age youth are not going to the polls.

The Bogalusa Voters League must continue its voter registration efforts.

The building burned to the ground. But, the organization is the officers and the bylaws. The work will continue.

They might need some help. What about you?

What is your five-year plan?

Write it down. Step-by-step.

Let me tell you! One of my nieces had a plan.

Yes, she did. She planned to become a prenatal NURSE.

You know what happened. Let me tell you.

She waited until she got in the 12th grade to take the ACT.

She made a 19. But the school her great uncle James Meredith risk his to integrate in 1960 changed its policies while she was in high school. She needed a 21 on the ACT to get in NURSING School. Some medical fields in our state require students make a 24.

Policies change. Elected officials make policies. The vote is powerful. The laws and public policies effect every aspect of our lives from the condition of our local library to the availability of books for children enrolled in public schools.

One lady in my hometown told me her daughter and two other girls were sharing the same science textbook and all of them were flunking.

Didn't we march about that in the 20th century?

Malcolm X said, ***the vote is more powerful than the dollar bill***.

Is it fair to say the struggle continues?

"Hands Up Don't Shoot" was the rallying cry after Mike Brown was shot to death in the streets of Ferguson.

When Attorney General Eric Holden went to Ferguson and denounced the city's Debtor's Prison, municipalities across the country had to shut down their Debtor's Prison.

The U.S. Supreme Court banned Debtor's Prisons in 1974.

Are you serious. Municipalities were breaking federal laws.

My hometown was sued last year. Now if a citizen can't pay a traffic fine they get to make a payment arrangement rather than go to jail and work off the fine doing community service.

The Affordable Care Act and shutting down debtor's prison are two significant achievements of the Obama administration.

Even through over 20 million additional Americans have health insurance today the U.S. Senate took the first step to repeal the Affordable Care Act known as Obamacare Thursday.

The struggle continues. We need drum majors for JUSTICE.

We must stop the **school-to-prison pipe-line**.

How? School preparation, give book gifts instead of toys.

How? Give our children chores. Teach them the value of hard work.

How! My uncle proposes we teach every Black male the Ten Commandments and the Golden Rule by age five (5).

The Golden Rule (**Do until others as you would have them do until you**).

The Golden Rule teaches us to have agape love for one another.

Agape love dictates a nurse feed a bedridden patience HOT food.

No, No, Luke warm won't do. Walk that tray to the microwave.

Agape love dictates children respect their parents, their elders, and authority.

Practice, sacrifice, dedication. The King of Pop - Michael Jackson – understood that "practice makes perfect"

He use to practice his dance moves until his legs hurt.

His ***Thriller*** album has sold over a Billion copies.

The Bogalusa Voters League must continue its voter registration efforts. I want to thank Emma Dixon for putting my name in the speaker's hat.

We are both members of a national multicultural organization called Rural Leadership Development Network which co-sponsored this event.

I want to thank the Bogalusa Voters League for allowing me to speak. Thank you for coming. I am honored to be standing in this historic church.

I was honored to walk on the ground where our elders stood tall and proud during the 20th century asking for better wages, better schools, and a diverse police department. I encourage you to support your local leadership.

Finally, my friend. I leave you with two of my favorite quotes of my uncle James Meredith.

You should let no excuse stand in your way.
Life is like a game of chess. You must plan every move.

Yesterday matters--The future must be planned.
Thank you.

Campaign to form the **Friends of the Richard Wright Library**
1052 Maria Court • Jackson, MS 39204
601.372.0229 • meredithcmcgee@gmail.com
https://meredithetc.com/richard-wright-library/

https://www.facebook.com/campaign-to-form-a-friends-of-the Richard-Wright-Library

WE REPLACED THE **FRIENDS OF THE RICHARD WRIGHT LIBRARY CAMPAIGN** WITH THE **COMMUNITY LIBRARY INITIATIVE**

https://www.facebook.com/communty.library.ms

Jackson, Mississippi • Monday, December 19, 2016

Address to the Hinds County Board of Supervisors

Proactive Jacksonians seek to form the 1st ever Friends of the Richard Wright Library, but they were stopped in their tracks…

Good morning.

I am Meredith Coleman McGee, a citizen of District Five in Hinds County, of Ward Six in Jackson.

Thank you for the opportunity to discuss the dilemma we faced and why we launched the **Campaign to form the Friends of the Richard Wright Library**.

This Campaign seeks to challenge the **Jackson Hinds Library System's** policy articulated to me by Mrs. Patty Furr that the eight (8) libraries in Jackson can only have one Friends Group.

According to United for Libraries, Friends Groups include a core group of citizens who form for the sole purpose of raising funds to support a library branch.

The material distributed by the Mississippi Library Commission stated that grant money is mailed directly to library branches.

The group raises $50 to start-up because it cost $50 to file the bylaws with the Mississippi Secretary of State.

Once the group is formed and the paperwork is in order, an employee of the Mississippi Library Commission meets the core group of citizens at the library branch and trains them how to start raising funds.

The start-up process is simple. However, we were stopped in our tracks.

Mrs. Furr tried to persuade us to form a **Foundation** or to join the **Jackson Friends of the Library.** She even threw out a name. She said we could call it the **Richard Wright Library Literacy Foundation**.

I discussed these suggestions with the core group of citizens and we decided a Friends group would serve our purpose.

Mrs. Furr decided to give the **Jackson Friends of the Library** the task of deciding whether our group of citizens can form a second Library Friends group. The ideal that a VOLUNTEER board would decide the fate of another VOLUNTEER board seemed odd. Then all the delays appeared more like the military tactic of worrying an enemy into defeat because there was nothing welcoming about being told that our group would compete with the **Jackson Friends of the Library** for funds and confuse the public.

Based on letters, petitioner comments, and feedback from community residents, the PUBLIC is already confused, disappointed, and dismayed with the School System and the Jackson Hinds Library system.

Richard Wright is an icon. The Richard Wright Library is a public institution funded with our tax dollars. Richard Wright's love for reading made him an intellectual. His intellect gave him the knowledge to become a writer. His story is a testament of the power of BOOKS. His story can inspire others -over and over again-. **

My uncle Civil Right icon James Howard Meredith, a highly intelligent man, has written a stack of books. He determined that our race needs to produce "Intellectual Giants."

He is also one who loves to read. According to his book, ***What every Black Family Ought to Know About the Library***, libraries need resources to reach the disadvantaged population and that man's knowledge has been stored in libraries for over 6,000 years.

His work also documented the history of how libraries have neglected the disadvantaged population.

WEB Dubois, a Black scholar, proposed that our race needs a "Talented Tenth." Intellect is acquired via books, audio books, documentary films, and etc.

I am an avid book lover. That's why I am more concerned about books than potholes. The children who go to the Richard Wright Library do not know his story. His story is important and inspirational.

As I understand history, Richard Wright was a boy 80 years ago. As a child, he loved to read. He probably obtained books from what citizens describe as the "Black Library." Citizen interviews noted that we had a library on Mill Street and one of Whitfield Mill Rd.

While in line at Walmart, Ms. Gloria said to me, "I started going to the library on Mill Street at age 10 in 1953. We didn't have many books in our library but we read whatever we could. I still like to read," she said.

Back to Richard Wright's story. He attended the Smith Robertson School on Bloom Street in the Farish Street Historic District. He completed the 8th grade and was valedictorian of his class. He probably used the same library Ms. Gloria used.

But, neither one of them could use the library on State Street which housed the largest collection of books during segregation. But, reading whatever they could read changed their life. Reading gives people a constructive hobby if nothing else.

Reading took Richard Wright to places he would never have imagined reaching. Growing up, his family was poor. Nevertheless, at age 14, Richard wrote a short story which was published by the Southern Register, a Black newspaper on Farish Street.

In the 1920s, Richard Wright, the son of a maid was a disadvantaged Black boy. Today, I speak for the disadvantaged. Because I believe, our library system in on the wrong side of history and that this body and board can put this situation in order.

My oldest brother Bobby had dyslexia. The words on the pages merged. He could barely read. His friend told me last week that when they were teenagers. Bobby would come in their house and change the TV to MS Public TV and persuade them to watch a documentary instead of "Good Times" because they could read and he couldn't.

My niece graduated from Lanier High School, her goal was to become a nurse. She made a 19 on the ACT. Her great uncle integrated Ole Miss but she, like many JPS graduates cannot get into four year colleges.

Reading will solve some of these problems.

- A teen in our neighborhood, signed the Campaign petition. She said she takes her 10-year-old brother to the Richard Wright Library but he is discouraged because he loves to read and it's hard for him to find books that interest him now.
- Two Middle school boys said their mother takes them to the library in Byram.
- One south Jackson mother said she passes by the Richard Wright Library and drives to the Eudora Welty Library where there are more resources.
- Patrons also complain that there is not enough parking space at the Richard Wright Library during school hours.

May I indulge you for another minute, two minutes.

I have been going to the Richard Wright Library for 18 years. A lot has changed. The library has and is a great resource to citizens and it use to support small businesses.

May I point out that in 2002, I was laid off and I started a homebased business (known also as a micro business).

I walked inside the Richard Wright Library and asked my librarian if I could hang my beautiful business flyer on the bulletin board.

The director hung my flyer on the board and it took me 30 days to get my first customer.

He was a white male who needed someone to type his Civil War story about the Confederate Army's use of Submarines.

You may find this strange, but my flyers stayed on the bulletin board for over eight years and landed me lots of customers who live in my community.

I could go to the library and get a flyer about a new book, or a new business, or an event in my community. When I tell you, there was much more traffic at our library in those days. Now, the library only post non-profit businesses flyers. For-profit businesses pay taxes.

Our library can do so much more for our community. It is struggling. The Richard Wright Library needs funds for more programs. We want to be friends of our library branch. Are you going to let us?

OUR CORE GROUP: Ercilla Hendrix, wife of Ward 6 Councilman Tyrone Hendrix; Starkishia Rountree, Healthcare Professional, Author, mother of four; Loretha Wallace, mother of four, grandmother of 11; Businessman Timothy Stamps, Stamps Superburger; Attorney Jovaunda Smith, and others.

Thank you.
Happy Holidays

Note: The board president informed me that the Hinds County Board's body did not have the authority to help our group. A hinds county lawyer informed me to go to the Mississippi Library Commission and the Mississippi Library Commission said they were not the proper body to assist us. Therefore some of the group members launched the Community Library Initiative to create a Community Library or Libraries in our community to address our literacy and other library needs.

Make that money woman
Meredith Coleman McGee, Presenter
Rural Development Leadership Network

Make that money woman
Take your products to the market
Sell them at the perfect price
Not too low
Not too high
Sell them at a price that is right
Know your market
Investigate
Ask questions
Talk to potential buyers
I have books.
Softcover $10, $14
Hardback - $44, a textbook, $15
Rare limited print, leatherbound edition - $250
Make that money woman.
Take your services to the people.
How much will you charge for your services?
- consultant services
- life coach will you charge $45 or $65 per hour?
- small business consultant - $45 or $100 per hour?
Writing services - $45 or 85 per hour?
Will you obtain speaker honorarium fees - $150, 5K, 10K
Make that money woman!

Q & A

CDW 61 Women's Economic Empowerment in the Changing World of Work, March 14-18, 2017.

Ending Violence Against Women: Prevention and Response to Femicide/Gender-Related Killings of Women

SOMETHING WRITTEN

Rome wasn't built over night – it grew over years of toil and so will a new business.
Meredith C. McGee

This chapter contains a collection of articles and writings by the author from 1994 to 2018. McGee contributed the following article about the late Percy King and Jason Birtfield to the Jackson Advocate which is the oldest black owned newspaper in Mississippi in January of 2018. McGee started writing professionally for this news outlet in December of 1993 under the guidance of the late Charles Tisdale and his wife Alice Thomas-Tisdale.

Mississippi's beloved 'Snakeman' Percy King

By Meredith C. McGee, Jackson Advocate, Contributing Writer

Friday, January 19, 2018, around 12:30 p.m., a gunman took the lives of Percy King, age 57, and his 19-year-old mentee, Jarvis Jawon Birtfield in King's front yard on Scott St., a-skip-and-hop from Cherry Grove M.B. Church and two blocks south of Martin Luther King Dr.

Balloons anchored a make shift memorial and candles were burning on the curve of the street in front of Percy King's house Wednesday, afternoon, January 24th at press time. Several empty glass cages which once housed Percy King's exotic pets were in the yard. The pets were recently removed by Wildlife authorities.

Percy King was a self-employed entertainer. Neighborhood parents booked him for birthday parties. He entertained church and civic groups across the state too.

Every year in October, Percy King displayed his private collection of exotic animals at the State Fair in Jackson. He charged visitors a $1 admission fee. “Percy use to encourage children to touch the animals so they would not be afraid,” Willie Ann Stewart, his neighbor of 34 years recalled.

Percy kept beautiful peacocks and other animals in his yard before he was hired to work at the zoo. “Even when Percy was a young man, Mrs. Lucille, his mother, allowed him to have a mini zoo in the back yard,” Stewart said. “Percy taught himself most of the knowledge he had about animals,” she added. Hence, Percy had animal skills when he joined the Jackson Zoo’s staff.

“Percy was a peacemaker. If he saw two people arguing in the street, he would say, “Don’t ya’ll do that!” Stewart declared. According to Stewart, Percy King would go out of his way to find a resolution to keep peace. “Percy was one of the best neighbors anyone could ever dream of having,” Stewart declared.

Quincy King, a great nephew of Percy King recalled with a warm smile, “My Uncle Percy use to ride around with a big python in his Green Dodge Caravan.” Percy King had pet snakes and his public love for snakes garnered him the pet name – “Snakeman.” Pythons which are native to Africa, Asia, and Australia are among the largest snakes in the world.

"Children loved taking pictures with the animals when they finished the tour at the fair," Quincy King added. Quincy is the grandson of Ricky King. The late Ricky and Bo King started the King Brother's Tire Shop on Medgar Evers Blvd years ago. Quincy is the third generation of Kings in the tire business.

Quincy King, King Brother's

Percy served on the Jackson Zoo's Board of Directors. He formerly was a zookeeper for the City of Jackson from 1997 to 2011.

Mt. Vision Baptist Church on Martin Luther King Dr. has hosted the MLK Program for Councilman Kenneth I. Stokes for over 20 years. Councilman Stokes knows the entire King Family. Percy's father Rev. Leroy King was a longtime pastor of the church.

"Percy was the baby of the family," Stokes noted. "Percy King was a community minded, Christian soldier. He spent years, years, and years trying to help people."

"The City of Jackson and the State of Mississippi loss a champion of peace and one who understood animals," Stokes proclaimed.

Councilman Stokes remembered receiving a call from a woman known as 'Big Ma' on Mark St. about a snake in the yard which was near King Brother's Tires. Percy worked at the tire shop with his older brothers. He heard about the snake and tried to help 'Big

Ma' but was too late. She emptied three guns on the snake before Percy arrived," Councilman Stokes fondly recalled.

One of Percy King's classmates, RaMona Alexander, from Lanier High School was in the school's String Orchestra with Percy. "He played the violin and I played the cello. He was a very nice guy. He and all of his brothers were talented musicians," she stated.

Tiffany Day Duncan, one of Percy's neighbors, recalled that he once played a joke on her while she was in the yard of the empty house next door picking up paper and cleaning the yard. He said excitedly, "Watch your step! One of my snakes is over there!" When Percy laughed, Duncan realized he was joking around.

"People loved Percy. He had a calm disposition," Stokes added. Duncan agreed, "Percy was always happy."

Percy King was impressive; his personality has ascended into the clouds, but his memory lives on. Stewart said with deep sincerity, "Percy is truly going to be missed."

The public can view Percy King's body Friday, January 26th from 8 a.m. to 8 p.m. at Westhaven Funeral Home on Robinson St. Westhaven is also handling Birtfield's body.

The funeral service is also open to the public. It will be held at 11:00 a.m. at 3420 Albermarle Road at Morning Star Baptist Church in Jackson.

Rest in Heaven

Percy Alehman King - July 20, 1960 – Jan. 19, 2018
Jarvis Jawon Birtfield - Nov. 18, 1998- Jan. 19, 2018

PTA at Mississippi's top school is raising funds to accommodate historic name change

By Meredith C. McGee, Jackson Advocate, Contributing Writer

Pupils and parents learned civic and history lessons from the vetting process to switch a Jackson, Mississippi school named for Confederate President Jefferson Davis to a name that will honor President Barack Obama, the nation's first president of Kenyan American descent.

Anitra and Sam Bender

Sam Bender, a Davis Magnet International Baccalaureate Elementary School fifth grader, who is Black, said with conviction, "Jefferson Davis was not a good name for our school because he was a Confederate soldier."

Jefferson Davis was a wealthy planter and a Mexican American war hero; he owned the Brierfield Plantation, in Davis Bend, Mississippi, south of Vicksburg. He amassed a fortune from the production of cotton using the free labor of his African slaves. While making a public comment at the Jackson School Board Meeting, October 18, 2017, Janelle Hannah Jefferson, PTA President, announced that students and stakeholders decided to rename the school and the board officially sanctioned the name change.

According to Ms. Jefferson, every class participated in the name change voting process. Students conducted research and submitted recommended names. Each class voted on name slots. On October 5th, the name Barack Obama fared well over his four competitors and his name was selected.

Jefferson's two children, Jacob, a 3rd grader, and Brooklynn, a 2nd grader, were among the 266 pupils who submitted hand ballots. "Around 150 parents submitted hand ballots on October 5th," Jefferson noted.

"Philanthropists have already reached out to us offering donations to cover the cost of changing the name," Jefferson added.

In fact, Davis, an A+ rated school, is the highest rated school in the state which is unfortunately not the case of most of the schools in Jackson Public School's failing school district. Jackson Public School's racial makeup is 97.51% African American, 1.83% White, 0.45% Hispanic, 0.18% Asian, and 0.03% Native American. The school's success is attributed to its outstanding teaching practices and to the great leadership of the school's principal, Kathleen Grigsby.

Davis is located in the heart of downtown on Congress St. across the street from the birthplace of Mississippi writer Eudora Welty and down the street from Greenwood Cemetery which was established in 1822, via a land grant, a year after the city's formation. The cemetery is the resting place of at least six Confederate generals and hundreds of Confederate soldiers.

Sam's mother, Anitra Bender, learned a history lesson too. Anitra said, "I learned that Jefferson Davis and Pres. Barack Obama are distant relatives."

Sam said with conviction, "Jefferson Davis was picked to become the President of the Confederacy (1861-1865) because he came up with the best attack idea for Rebel soldiers to use against Union soldiers." Sam added, "He wanted to take over the land."

Sam declared, "Jefferson Davis was a very great military leader. He was very nervous as a president." At the end of the Civil War, Jefferson Davis was charged with treason, arrested, and imprisoned for two years. Jefferson Davis and other Confederate leaders eventually obtained presidential pardons.

The name change marks the beginning of an era when public protest has wielded citizens enough energy and power to attack the power structures which placed the statues of White Supremacist like Jefferson Davis and Robert E. Lee in the public space.

Earlier this year, May 11, 2017, the Jefferson Davis statue on Canal St. and Jefferson Davis Parkway in New Orleans was removed. The statue was erected 106 years ago at a time when Blacks and women were disenfranchised in this country.

For Black Mississippians removing the name Jefferson Davis from a school in the Capital City is one step toward cleansing the public space of White Supremacy idolatry. However, the name change is not a cure all. One of Mississippi's 82 counties is named for Jefferson Davis. There is a Jefferson Davis Community Hospital in Prentiss, Mississippi too.

The stage in Davis's school auditorium has two flag poles. The American flag hangs on the pole in the left corner, while the Confederate flag hangs on the flag pole in the right corner.

Jefferson declared, "I was very proud of the research process the students went through to get us to this point." She added, "I was very happy to be a part of the renaming of the school." Two of her four children participated in their school's election and witnessed the power of democracy.

The school's renaming news reached every corner of the country. Stories were reported in the *Washington Post*, the *New York Times*, the *Huffington Post*, *Miss Today*, CNN, NBC, AP… the news appeared in 100s of news outlets.

National headlines: *Jefferson Davis out, Barack Obama in at Mississippi elementary school, Mississippi School Drops Jefferson Davis Moniker to Honor Barack Obama, School honoring Confederate icon to be renamed after Barack Obama…*

Sam Bender said, "Barack Obama represents a nice and kind leader." Sam said, "You should treat others the way you want to be treated." The voting and civic lessons didn't inspire Sam to become a politician like Pres. Barack Obama. Sam is inspired to become a great athlete. He happily announced, "I want to be a basketball player like Kevin Durant."

It is highly likely that this transformative school will produce future community advocates and politicians. Fourth and fifth graders campaigned like pros. One pupil produced a power point presentation and persuaded his peers to remember the slogan – Yes we can! They did.

Last month, the pupils studied history and voted to replace their school's name with a namesake that makes sense to them. Change is progress! Pure and simple!

In the end, perhaps school legend will remember Farah, a former Davis student, who initially challenged her school's name in 2013 while she was in the 4th grade. Farah, an avid reader, read a book about Jefferson Davis. Farah was not proud of the general's legacy.

The children's history awakening empowered them! Reading is powerful!

The PTA is now raising funds for a new school sign BARACK OBAMA IB SCHOOL and other memorabilia. Please mail donations to:

Obama Magnet PTA
PO Box 2391
Jackson, MS 39225

Send online donations to paypal.me/ObamaMagnetPTA or

https://www.facebook.com/BOESPTA/ Facebook page

Authors face discrimination when attempting to get published in MS

By Meredith C. McGee, Jackson Advocate, Contributing Writer

After college, I dreamed of becoming an author. At that time, I was an avid fiction reader. Today, I love reading memoirs and biographies about Black people, but I also appreciate the works of authors from other ethnic groups. While Richard Wright, Alice Walker, and J California Cooper are great writers, Toni Morrison is my favorite.

I learned that books are very powerful art forms because the fiction books I read when I was younger influenced me to read nonfiction books. Books introduce readers to people, historical events, information, and places.

Twenty years after the idea to become an author captured my imagination, I joined the mere one percent of book publishers who identify as Black in this nation and started a small press and became a publisher and a published author.

At the same time, after persevering past 16 rejection letters, I obtained a contract to publish a biography with a commercial publisher. In essence, I was able to witness the marketing power of a large book publisher and have since attempted to maneuver some of its marketing strategies. In starting a small press, I desired to take great books to the marketplace.

So far, we have published 15 book titles and they all stand tall and firm in their genres.

In September of 2017, I decided to submit six Meredith Etc book titles by Mississippi writers to the Mississippi Library Commission's database to expose the books to librarians and book lovers who are looking for books by Mississippians.

There was a hint of negativity from Miss Mellon from the start. She informed me via telephone that she would review the books to see if they were a right fit to be included in the agency's database. She told me upfront that they could donate the books to the public library if they were not accepted.

I thought about it, and I suggested that if the books were not good enough to be included in the database, I would prefer to pick them up so we could sell them. You see, we were donating our books to the agency's database as a marketing tool and for exposure.

We choose writing as a career path rather than as a hobby.

On the 26th of September, Miss Mellon called me and explained that all six of our books were rejected because they did not have book reviews from national outlets such as Publishers Weekly or Kirkus Reviews. She offered to ship them to me.

A few days later, I received a box with the books *Nashida: Visits the Mississippi State Capitol*, *Starkishia: Estrella*, *Death by Association* Vol. 1 *Retaliation* Vol. 2 *Deception*, *Mary's Story & Song*, *Social Justice and Christianity*, and *Woman Preach* from Ally Mellon, the Information Services Director, for the Mississippi Library Commission.

We were injured. We had searched the database before we submitted our books. Most of the books in the database had book reviews from Mississippi newspaper. Very few books had been reviewed by national outlets such as *The New York Times*.

One thing was apparent; we had been the victims of discrimination. So for us, Miss Mellon is the great gatekeeper who rejected our membership, so to speak, in the club (Mississippi online and physical marketplace).

Author Mary Haralson Coleman declared, “Unfair gatekeepers hurt us all.”

We were required to stand up to a different standard than other authors many of them were our white counterparts. Our books were required to have national reviews while some writers listed in the database did not even have a Mississippi newspaper review.

Three of our books were listed in the Mississippi Department of Archives and History’s (which list nonfiction) database as well as were available in reading rooms at the Library of Congress in Washington, DC. *Mary’s Story & Song* had reviews from the *Jackson Advocate* and the *Delta Democrat Times.*

Starkishia, Author, *Starkishia: Estrella* said, “It's ashamed that in 2017, institutionalized racism still exits. As an author, I am deeply offended by the actions of Ally Mellon who is in a position to help authors advance but choose to discriminate on the basis of race and economic class. In my opinion, closing the door in our faces, even when it's done with seemingly kind words and a smile, is the same as blatantly saying our work isn't good enough,” Starkishia is also the co-author of *Mary’s Story & Song*.

Being listed in these various databases has helped us obtain library sales.

Support local Black authors; buy our books; give us an honest review and a leg up in our craft.

Meredith C. McGee is the publisher and acquisition editor of Meredith Etc. Visit their online bookstore for more information about their books www.meredithetc.com.

The article below featured participants and the winners of a talent show which was hosted by MGT Entertainment at the Mediterranean Fish & Grill in Ridgeland, MS July 22, 2012.

Mississippi's Got Talent

By Meredith C. McGee, Jackson Advocate, Contributing Writer

Three middle age African American male judges rendered a tie to 3 out of 12 acts, who performed at MGT Entertainment's 12th Talent Show in a packed house at The Mediterranean Fish & Grill in Ridgeland, Mississippi on Sunday, July 22, 2012.

Categories to select the finalist included but were not limited to originality and stage presence. As is the custom at Amateur Night at the Apollo Theatre, Bessie the event organizer held her hand over the head of each finalist and let the audience pick the winners.

The loudest roars were rendered to a well deserving rapper named Chip, who came in 1st place and walked away with a trophy and the largest cash price. He and the other winners O. Jones and Diamond Monae will appear on MGT Live which airs on channel 18 via Comcast Cable at 1:30 am Thursday morning and 8:30 pm Friday night.

No performers were booed off the stage. In fact, all 12 acts, most of which were youth, had it together; one female R&B soloist named Destiny rocked the house singing about the drama in a young woman's life.

Aljajuan Bell known as AMB has been performing in churches and clubs since he was 14. A female from the audience was escorted on stage, seated and crowned a queen during his act. AMB said, "At first I was doing worldly music then the Lord made a change in life. Now I use my music to glorify God and to inspire people." He added, "I don't use women as sex toys."

Brandon Hampton (Black Dove) Angela Wilson, Aljajuan Bell (AMB), Alverrecheo Bell

Lisa Starr Cory Armstrong AMB

I want to inspire them to be independent and achieve their goals in the music industry without lowering their standards." AMB is a CNA at Mississippi State Hospital; he dreams of becoming an entertainment professionally and has made strides. "I have a song on Derek Martin's album *Up Next*," he said humbly. His debut album *The Light of the World* will be released through Strictly Positive Entertainment.

Chip 1st Place Winner

O. Jones 2nd Place Winner

The Artist Known as Two Three & Young Ensane

The Artist Known as Two Three (William E. McGee III) is a sophomore at JSU pursuing a degree in Sociology. He works for Kraft Foods as a merchandiser, but still finds time for musical endeavors with his right hand man, Roderick Whitley (Young Ensane). "We met a few years ago as co-workers at a local Piggly

Wiggly, and instantly became friends after finding out we both had a passion for music," Two Three noted. Shortly afterward, the two formed a group called Simply Talented.

Two three expressed his ambitions with his lyrics,

> On the road to riches, but it couldn't come sooner, trying to make the money spread, spread like a rumor!
> You can see my swagger's bright. I'm hungry for success and I'm not trying to lose my appetite!

Young Ensane exerted confidence in his group's talent when he spit,

> Mind sharp on the beat like blade tips, you're looking at the sky while we fly high in spaceships!

Courtney Slaughter, a songwriter and poetic lyricist, is a student at USM majoring in Sports Medicine. She started writing poetry in middle school. She recalled, "I wrote how I felt." In high school she added hooks to her poems and turned them into songs. Her first performance was at the Multipurpose Center in Canton. She thinks the judges did a good job of picking the winners noting, "The performers who won were going hard at it." She wants to be successful in the music industry, but admitted, "School is my top priority."

Courtney was holding her own during the competition when she sang,

> I'm on the rise no looking down, listen to my words and not just the sound. When we first met you use to make me laugh.
>
> One plus one equals two but I guess you couldn't do the math.

Courtney Slaughter

Sip the Kid

"MGT Entertainment is always looking for new talent" Bessie stated. Contact MGT by becoming friends with Bessie on Facebook/bessieclayborn. Visit them online www.msgottalentproductions.com or call 601.291.6493.

Note: William E. and Meredith C. McGee are the parents of William E. McGee, III. He was a regular participant in MGT Entertainment's talent shows. He attended The Academic and Performing Arts Complex in middle school (Jackson Public School), was a Malone Scholar at St. Andrews Episcopal High School (Ridgeland, MS), and was the recipient of a Presidential Scholarship to Jackson State University (Jackson, MS). We appreciate MGT because it provides a positive outlet to our city's youth.

College grads end up with more than just a diploma in their hands

Bills, bills and more bills

Many college graduates have tossed their hats in the air, celebrated, and are now looking for high salaried positions to help them pay off their gigantic student loan debt.

Timothy Norris, a Jackson State University graduate, obtained a contract for employment a few months ago with Holmes County School District in his field as a Psychometrist, Ed.S where he serves as a consultant, and counsels and provides psychometrically sound educational student assessments. Norris completed an internship with St. Dominic Hospital and had to obtain a license before landing a job in his field. “I was disappointed after obtaining a specialist degree to have to take the praxis 1 test as a prerequisite to employment,” Norris noted.

The success of graduates to obtain high wage jobs is pertinent because low skill jobs will not allot the discretionary income necessary to pay student loan debt. According to the College of Access & Success, student indebtedness has increased since the 1990s, and the class of 2010 had an average of $25,250 in student debt which exceeded credit-card debt for the first time.

An anonymous Mississippi College graduate who obtained a specialist degree in Educational Leadership has accumulated nearly $75,000 in student loan debt. She pays $380 per month for her undergraduate college debt for which she selected a 20-year repayment option. Her second loan associated with her masters degree is $250 a month. Since the cost of living has risen drastically, she has been getting her second loan deferred. In addition, she borrowed $25,000 to complete a specialist degree. She has not started paying her third loan yet, but her cumulative payment could exceed $800 per month, if her debt is not consolidated.

She has been teaching for over a decade, but declared, “I can’t afford to pay my student loan debt off on my annual teacher’s salary.” She has juggled her debt so long, until she is pessimistic claiming, “I may end up taking some of my college debt with me to my grave.” Her employer, Jackson Public Schools, has a freeze on hiring which is a stumbling block to her goal of increasing her income by becoming an assistant principal or a principal. She proposed, “They need to just wipe out all the student loans.”

Students entering college can enroll in a junior college for their first two years and borrow the bear basics to reduce college indebtedness. Above all else, graduates should make every effort to pay off their student loans. Deferments carry stiff fees, which only prolongs debt. Student loan default can be a catastrophe because wages could be garnished, tax refund money taken, and property confiscated, which could blemish credit, making it harder to get jobs or professional licenses.

Galloway students receive sound advice from Merritt

8 of the school's Gifted Program students. Calla in the white dress.

Galloway Elementary School, located on Idlewild Street in Jackson, Mississippi, promoted 33 fifth graders May 25, 2012.

Calla Ridgeway, the only girl out of nine in the Gifted Program, received twelve awards, some of which included *The Most Intellectual Girl, Most Books Read During Free Time,* and *Awesome Artist Award.*

Ridgeway, who has cared for and loved pets since she was a toddler, wants to someday become a veterinarian. She has her maternal, great uncle James H. Meredith to thank for the opportunity to pursue this field. For, it was he who broke down barriers nearly 50 years ago in Mississippi which prohibited blacks for studying medical, legal, and other advance degrees at state colleges.

Ridgeway introduced the guest speaker, LaToya Merritt, J.D., a partner of Phelps & Dunbar LLC., who told the fifth graders, "A lot is expected of you; continue to do your best." She also noted, "Learning is continuous."

Erica Gee-Bradley, the school's principal, provided a message which she called "real talk" to the audience. She admonished parents to embrace the old adage - *It takes a village to raise a child* condemning the ideology - *You get your child. I'll get mine.*

Gee-Bradley said, "I've got to talk to this class a little different from other classes." Looking directly at the fifth grade class she said, "Respect yourselves and respect others. Don't try to grow up to fast. Be a little girl. Be a little boy." She declared "Girls cover up! Nobody wants a gift that has already been open. Young ladies are the queens of the earth. Boys! Respect the female. A female brought you into this world." She challenged the students to learn how to wash and iron their clothes, and asked them not to imitate everything they hear celebrities, rappers, and reality television actors say because some of them have been walking around sounding foolish emulating foolishness.

Gee-Bradley acknowledged the bravery of one fifth grader, Johnnie Smith, who became the Jr. Assistant Principal to help the school enforce disciplinary infractions. Johnnie called meetings to discuss problems and strategies, and recruited five other fifth graders and assigned them to various hall monitoring duties. Smith and his student team were rewarded monetary and or other gifts for their service.

The 5th Grade Boys Choir, the 5th Grade Class Choir, and the awardees gave the audience a glimpse of the multiple talents the students' possess. Hopefully this college class of 2019 will take heed to the "real talk" presented by Gee-Bradley, and remember the words of Merritt, "Your success won't be easy, but it will be worth the effort and hard work you put into it."

Ridgeway, the Valedictorian of her class, is spending the summer with her father Calvin Ridgeway in Griffin, Georgia. Her mother Willa Ridgeway was a former JPS substitute teacher. Her grandmother, a major figure in her life, Hazel Janell Meredith, known as Hazel Hall, is the author of *My Brother J-Boy* and co-author of *A Story About James H. Meredith, A Civil Rights Leader* which are children books on James H. Meredith www.shopheirs.com [see www.meredithetc.com too].

The school's theme "Success is failure turned inside out," is a reminder to the children to stay in the race. Johnnie Smith, who stopped violating school rules and became a force to be reckoned with as a Jr. Assistant Principal and Hall Monitor, is an example of progress - *real talk.*

Note: At the end of the summer break, Calla asked her Aunt Meredith, "Why did you put me in the paper?"

Her Uncle Will replied, "Because you did something great."

Calla complained, "But I didn't want anyone to see me."

Historic walk teaches basic principle

Front: Fred Watson and James Meredith
Back: Pastor Church Meador and Senturian DuReaux

James H. Meredith, who integrated Ole Miss on September 30, 1962, accompanied by a small group of supporters, launched a historic walk from the Tennessee/Mississippi state line Saturday May 25, 2012 at 10 am on Highway 51. The message for The Walk for Education and Truth is listed below:

1. Only the family of God can solve the problems of our time.

2. The Bible says, "You should train up a child in the way he should go, and when he is old he will not depart from it."
3. The African proverb says, "It takes a whole community to raise a child."
4. God's plan is that every church in Mississippi should take responsibility for every child born within two miles of the church.
5. The church should keep a record of each child from birth to age 21.

Everyone is welcome to join the walk. Meredith extended a special invitation to women over 65, veterans, and Ole Miss students and alumni.

James Meredith's granddaughters Jameria and Janae posed for a fun picture during a break.

James Meredith's walk for education and truth reaches the Jackson Area June 10-13, 2012.

James Meredith and his granddaughter Jameria Knight in front

June 10 the walk will begin at the Canton, MS city limit sign at 4 p.m. on Hwy 51 N.

June 11 the walk will begin in Madison on Hwy 51 in front of Krogers at 4 pm

June 12 the walk will begin in Tougaloo at County Line Rd and State Street at 4 p.m.

June 13 the walk will begin at 4 pm in Jackson in the Fondren District at Duling School on State St. and will end at the Old State Capital on Street St.

Sykes honors 74 students headed to middle school

Eric Hart (2nd on right in white shirt)

Sykes Elementary School which has a student body of 471 was one of 39 public schools in the City of Jackson to facilitate Award Day festivities. The event honored 74 fifth graders who were advancing to middle school.

Of note was Eric Hart, a gifted African American male with a 3.5 GPA. As a result of his dedication to learning, Eric is already testing on the eighth grade level, and took home more awards than any of his classmates. His proud father, Eric Hart, jumped to his feet and yelled congratulatory words of praise a dozen times.

During the evening after school studying is a priority, and television is forbidden, a practice which is also enforced in the White House by President and Mrs. Obama.

Eric's mother, Kenya Hart said, "Eric builds small motors," which is significant since he aspires to become an architect. Eric's grandmother, Geneva Brooks, an assistant teacher at Sykes, is the force behind his academic success. Brooks noted, "We get support from the school. Some teachers stay late at no charge to tutor students." This summer, as is customary, Eric's grandmother will prepare him for the next grade level using grade appropriate workbooks.

Eric's classmate, Angelica Reynolds, a Gifted Program participant, received a Creative Writing Award. "We write about superheroes, Martin Luther King Jr., poems, haiku, and rhymes." she noted. Angelica has been taught African American and Hispanic roots by her parents, Rufus and Velet Sampson. "Angelica knows that her father's ancestors were forbidden by law to learn how to read and write during slavery and she doesn't take for granted the freedom she has today. "I feel that everyone has the right to say what they feel and write it down and to express their true feelings," she proclaimed. This summer Angelica is completing a collection of poems and short stories, which she plans to publish in the near future.

The school's Principal, Eloise Jones says, "I hope parent meeting and conference participation will increase next year, because research indicates children are more academically successful when parents are involved." However she is concerned for the outgoing students noting, "Parent involvement tends to decline the older children become."

The Award Day program speaker, Whiten Middle School Principal Anthony Moore, discouraged students from succumbing to peer pressure. He said, "You're headed to middle school next year. You'll be in the midst of 7th, 8th, and 9th graders. Don't let any of them tell you what to do. Listen to your parents and teachers."

Twenty-four year old Tommie Mabry, an ISS instruction at Whiten walked briskly across the auditorium floor revealing several of his 54 tattoos and captivated the audience with his testimony. Mabry grew up in the Midtown community known as the North End. "I was in the fifth grade when I first got locked up," he professed. "We were trying to be cool and trying to fit in." he admitted. During his turbulent youth, Mabry defied authority, and was expelled from every elementary and middle school in Jackson. His criminal activity elevated from petty thief to strong arm robbery, carjacking, and selling drugs.

Tommie Mabry with Darlene D. Collier - Photo by Cyrus Webb

In high school Mabry travelled with the basketball team which gave him an outlet from his community; remarkable, he turned his life completely around after being shot in the 12th grade. Though he had been predicted to fail, Mabry was crowned *Mr. Tougaloo* and completed college. He is the author of *A Dark Journey to a Light Future*. Mabry hopes his story will encourage students to take education seriously noting, "There is nothing dumb about being smart."

Sykes Elementary School is on academic watch but Jones is confident the school is heading in the right direction because she has a dedicated staff. Great possibilities are awaiting Eric,

Angelica, and even the average students. Mabry is proof that it is never too late to get on track.

Money, fees, and your future

By Meredith C. McGee, Jackson Advocate, Contributing Writer

The rising cost of living and the poor economy have dampened the prospects for many to establish a future financial underpinning.

Some time ago, one of my former employers matched 401 (k) plan contributions dollar for dollar, but, after one year and 11 months of employment, three workers and I were laid off within 30 days of becoming vested in our retirement program. Hence, our employer's matching funds were forfeited the day we were laid off.

Saving is really hard for individuals who are self-employed, and fewer and fewer companies provide retirement funds to employees. Gladys Hubbard, a self-employed beautician said, "I've been doing hair for 35 years. With this economy, retirement is not even an issue. I plan to work as long as I can and collect social security at age 62." Myra Bryant, who has worked for the same company for over 20 years said, "Our organization doesn't offer retirement plans." Bryant will approach retirement age in less than 15 years; she is now accumulating retirement funds without the support of her employer. According to 87 year old Beulah Thomas, she could not make ends meet with only her social security check even though her mortgage is paid off. She said, "I receive social security and two pension checks but, I wouldn't make it off only my social security check."

Interest rates for retirement accounts with small balances are not appealing. Wachovia is one of many banks that pay .1 percent interest for traditional saving and IRA accounts opened with less than $500. IRAs can be opened with $25 or less, and Wachovia will transfer monthly installments from a checking account into an IRA each month. However, be aware that if checking account funds are short any given month, the first NSF fee is $22 and additional fees are $35. To avoid NSF fees, account holders can opt-out of overdraft protection, which would stop funds from being transferred from a checking account if they are not immediately available. Opting-out of overdraft protection is relevant sense NSF fees are converted into profit for financial institutions and losses to account holders.

The interest rate on traditional retirement accounts range from .5 to 2.75 percent at Hope Community Credit Union. A minimum of $500 is required to open an IRA account with them. Banks and credit unions offer much higher earnings when individuals open retirement accounts with $1,000 or more. One thousand dollars can also purchase ROTH accounts, which offer tax breaks upon retirement or after age 59 when individuals are allowed to use funds without being penalized.

If you plan to take retirement funds from one institution and put them in an account at another institution, be warned of account closing fees which range from $75 to $95. It is cheaper to transfer funds. Transfer fees are $25 or so. Account holders are also hit with minimum account balance fees.

Oddly, The same bank that pays consumers .1 percent charges 29.99 percent in interest. Save regularly, expose funds to as much interest as possible, but don't let your financial institution deflate your money and future with fees.

Note: Some consumers are against opting out of overdraft protection from their checking account because they want protection for mortgage insurance, and notable drafts. However, opting out of debit card overdraft protection prevents consumers from being charged fees for trivial purchases. For example, banks charge fees if one uses a debit card to purchase an $8 car wash when he or she only has $7.99 in his or her account. Some consumers would rather pay the fee than to be denied purchasing power and embarrassed, while others would rather be embarrassed than to pay a $39 NSF fee for being short a penny.

200 miles for the poor and powerless

By Meredith C. McGee, Jackson Advocate, Contributing Writer

James Meredith's Historic 200 Mile Walk for the Poor kicked off, Sunday, May 24, 2009 in front of New Zion M.B. Church on Old Hwy. 61. S. in Tunica, MS.

Meredith shaking hands with a *Tunica Times* reporter

The weather was windy as a result of a recent rain when the walkers were lining up, but the sky cleared before 1:00 p.m. and a few minutes later, James Meredith and his wife, Dr. Judy Alsobrooks Meredith, led a group of walkers up Old Hwy. 61 S. to Hwy 4. As the walkers passed through the business district, the residents were given bookmarks that read, "I witnessed the Historic James Meredith 200 Mile Walk for the Poor Kick-Off.

Sis. Maureen Delaney and a friend had driven from Tutwiler to attend the kick-off. They and several local nuns caught up with the walk in progress. Motorists stopped and allowed the walkers to pass with great reverence. Tunica residents 40 years of age and older had heard of James Meredith, but even those who were not familiar with his place in Mississippi history had a lot of respect for his mission for the poor.

Most walk participants slowed down from exhaustion after walking five or six miles, but Meredith and his brother, Arthur Meredith, kept a steady pace ahead without stopping to take a break. They were physically fit for walking, having exercised regularly for years; when they were children they lived in a rural community in Kosciusko, MS and walked one hour to school and one hour from school. Though, Meredith broke down Mississippi's color barrier to higher learning in 1962, the poor in today's world do not always have access to a quality education, a reminder that the fight for a better world must continue.

A 10 or 12 mile walk was a breeze for Meredith, even at age 75. Most of the younger walkers took rest breaks and were driven in one of several cars close by to catch back up with the group. As the walkers passed the business district, they saw flat land occupied with scattered buildings, some abandoned, and others in good condition.

The children were captivated with the sight of road kill, which included a snake, a bird, a frog, and the skeleton bones of a dog. Many scenes were filmed by Clay Haskell and Dylan Nelson who travelled to Tunica from Los Angeles, CA to film the Kick-Off activities. Haskell and Nelson, owners of Other Paw Productions, LLC, are developing a film on James Meredith and his impact on Mississippi.

During an Evening Gathering in Senatobia, MS at the Lillian Garden Community Homecoming, Darmyra Perry said in her introduction of James Meredith, "Mr. Meredith is no stranger to us in North, MS." Perry went on to note some of Meredith's accomplishment including his Walk Against Fear which he launched 43 years ago. His importance is visually noticeable at the school he integrated to Perry's relatives, who currently attend Ole Miss, because Meredith is honored in the form of a Civil Rights Memorial where a life size 6'2 bronze statue stands depicting him walking.

Lillian Garden Community Homecoming participants

However, Meredith's page in the history books are becoming lost to a new generation of youth, who are not aware that he paved the way for blacks and non-whites to pursue medical and law degrees in the State of Mississippi when he integrated the University of Mississippi, October 1, 1962. Filmmaker, Emmanuel Alexandre Jr., a New York City resident, filmed the Evening Gathering in Senatobia. He is also developing a film on Meredith and hopes to expose more people James Meredith's life.

Perry believes *James Meredith's 200 Mile Walk for the Poor* will have a significant impact on the future of this state. Tate County residents agree. On Memorial Day, Meredith, a veteran, who served in the Air Force from 1952 -1960, was walking for the poor. Katherine Nelson, a Jackson resident said, "He [James

Meredith] is still pulling for us. He still has helping his people on his mind." Eighty-two year old, Nelson plans to join the Walk when it reaches Jackson. While communities await Meredith's arrival, historians are filming and writing his legacy.

Meredith C. McGee, a niece of James Meredith, is serving as the media coordinator for the Walk. She is a professional writer for Typing Solutions Résumés & Etc and the website administrator for Heirsskymallcom www.shopheirs.com visit www.meredithetc.com too.

Note: Haskell and Nelson's film on Meredith (*Mississippi Messiah*) is forthcoming; at the time of the printing of this http://www.indiegogo.com/projects/mississippi-messiah book the film makers were still excepting donations. Visit their trailer for more information.

Meredith on the Road

By Meredith C. McGee, Jackson Advocate, Contributing Writer

Teens hanging out on Hancock St. across from Tutwiler Funeral Home which handled Emmett Till's body in 1955.

James H. Meredith, first black University of Mississippi graduate, launched a Walk for the Poor, Sunday, May 24, 2009 on Old Hwy. 61 S. in Tunica, MS.

Meredith is walking in hopes of bringing attention to the plight of the poor. Since the Walk began, he has met with mayors, elected officers, clergy, community leaders, and talked one-on-one to citizens who live along highways 61, 4, 6, 49, and 49 W.

Monday evening he spoke to a crowd at Tutwiler Community Education Center hosted by Genether Miller Spurlock, Mayor of Tutwiler. Local residents and a group of Habitat for Humanity volunteers from Chicago who were rehabilitating a house in Cleveland, MS earlier that day were in attendance. Jerome Little, President, Tallahatchie County Board of Supervisors spoke during the program.

After Meredith concluded his speech, Eric Patten, Affiliate Coordinator, W. Tutwiler for Habitat, asked Meredith what he believes the Rich should do for the Poor? Meredith admitted to Patten that he had asked a hard question, and paused before giving a long answer that discussed the customs of slavery in ancient societies among other things. "Blacks were the only former slaves in the history of the world who didn't get a means of becoming productive and property to get back on their feet," Meredith said.

He also indicated that former slaves and their families lagged behind economically, in part, because they did not get 40 acres and a mule after being emancipated. He considers injustice and the lack of power to be another component of this complicated problem. Patten said, "I was confused by Mr. Meredith's complex answer but I asked a complex question. I agree with him that the problem will not be solved by the government and that the church should work with the community to improve the conditions of the poor. I don't believe welfare and government aid has or will ever solve the problem."

James Meredith talked with six female teenagers before he left town; they were congregated down the street from the Center in front of a vacant commercial building while he was giving his presentation. They came inside the Center afterward to meet him; he introduced them to Lenora Saulsberry, a medical doctor and native of Tutwiler, who was visiting her family. Meredith told Brittany Tyler to teach her baby the alphabets and how to count to 100 before she entered school and she too would have the opportunity to become a doctor like Saulsberry, who had picked cotton in a nearby field and attended Tutwiler Public Schools, before obtaining a bachelor degree from Tougaloo College and graduating from medical school.

Taccara Cohn, Ameba Williams, Brittany Tyler, and Desirae Smith

The Center and Tutwiler Funeral Home said a lot about the town, because these two buildings were the only occupied structures on Hancock Street. The dilapidated building next to the funeral home is the site where 14 year old, Emmitt Till's body was taken and remained in a closed casket until his mother (Mamie) had it moved to Chicago, IL where funeral home attendants opened the casket to reveal to the world how Tallahatchie County whites had brutally murdered her son for whistling at a white female store clerk. A tear dropped from Meredith's eye when he talked about the lie and cover-up surrounding Till's death.

According to Meredith, Christian Missionary work relating to the black community was dropped by the Mississippi Southern Baptists during the Second Reconstruction (1955-1966). "Southern Baptists are the only force that can decide on new policy for the black race because Mississippi has the strongest voice on the issue of race in America," he noted.

Giving the rising cost of gas and soaring interest rates, it is getting harder for poor people to climb out of debt and keep up. Hopefully, Meredith's attention to the conditions of the poor and

SCLC's upcoming Campaign against Poverty will influence those with power to use their voice to get elected officials to reform policies that stripe away assets, bound consumers to perpetual debt, and prevent people from having basic survival tools.

The walk ends at 11 a.m. Sunday, June 21, 2009 in Jackson, MS at First Baptist Church on State Street. Contact Meredith C. McGee to arrange a special meeting or to obtain the Walk for the Poor Meeting Schedule.

Last 2 miles of Meredith's Walk for the Poor

Bill Chandler, MIRA, James H. Meredith, Rep. Jim Evans

James Meredith led a small group of citizens from Mt. Helm Baptist Church on Church St. at 10 a.m. to First Baptist Church, which sits on a city block between President, College, Mississippi, and State Streets in downtown Jackson, MS.

Meredith's point was buried in an 11-page document which was printed on legal size paper. "I can't make people understand what I'm doing now unless, they understand our history," He proclaimed. The subject line of the cover page, dated May 15, 2007, stated: THE UNFINISHED AND SOCIAL MISSION OF THE MISSISSIPPI SOUTHERN BAPTIST.

Historically speaking, the black members of what is now known as Mt. Helm Baptist Church worshiped at First Baptist Church in the basement from 1835 – 1868. During slavery, blacks were required to worship in the presence of whites. In

1868, the black members were kicked out of First Baptist church because their worship service was too loud. A white member of the community named, Mr. Helm, donated the lot on the corner of Lamar and Church St. for the erection of a church to accommodate the service of the 300+ black members.

"The issue of Missionary duty to blacks was discussed at the Mississippi Southern Baptist Convention for 130 years and dropped after the so called Second Reconstruction (known as the Civil Rights movement)," Meredith said. His goal is now to get Mississippi Southern Baptists to complete their Christian Missionary work with the black race. Meredith claims the Southern Baptists are the only force in America that can wield new policy to improve conditions for the black race. "There is little need for the strong black male work force today since the machine and computer age. The black male is used now for sports and entertainment," Meredith added.

When Meredith and the walkers reached First Baptist Church they were not singing any group songs or carrying any signs; they were greeted cordially by security guards and welcomed inside by the ushers who were standing outside of heavy wooden doors on State St. which is the rear of the church. Meredith informed the ushers that he wanted to deliver his thesis to the minister. One of the ushers opened the door to allow him to enter. He took a step toward the door, and the camera crew [Other Paw Productions, LLC] and the walkers stepped behind him; he quickly reversed his steps and asked the guard to deliver the thesis.

Several church officials came outside and talked with Meredith and finally the pastor of the church emerged, who shook hands with Mr. Meredith, and invited them in for worship services. His offer was declined, and he accepted the thesis. While they were talking, former Jackson mayoral candidate Charlotte Reeves came outside and greeted Mr. Meredith, within moments, Reeves was confronted by one of the walkers who told her, "You need to tear it [commercial property on Monument near Bailey Ave.] down.[ii]"

As Meredith led the walkers up Mississippi St., Reeves appeared out of the side door on Mississippi St. with her husband to confront the woman who had criticized her commercial property. The woman insisted that Reeves property had no value to her community and Reeves disputed her. The woman became emotional and sung repeatedly as she walked back to Mt. Helm, "It aint' over to God say it is." She pointed at the State Capitol and sung to the governor and state legislatures.

Several of the walkers including Meredith had participated in SCLC's march the previous day. D.D. Finklea, a photographer from Atlanta, GA, videoed SCLC's Poor People's Campaign Kickoff in Jackson and Meredith's last leg of his Walk for the Poor. "I came home to record this history for my grandchildren," Finklea said.

An *Associated Press* reporter asked Meredith while he was sitting outside of the State Capitol with the SCLC demonstrators what he planned to accomplish. "ABC – 123," Meredith replied summing up his message to save those living in poverty today between birth and age five. "This is the whole thing," Meredith told another inquiring mind while handing him a bookmark which encourages parents, grandparents, and guardians to teach their children their ABCs and how to count to 100 at home before they enter school.

While demonstrators were in the streets of Mississippi, Iranians were dying in the street yelling, "Where is my vote." Floridians had cried the same cry in 2000 on American soil. The Supreme Court had silenced them. In the end, a democracy is ruled by the leader of the government and the judges. Blacks have progressed in society since Meredith integrated Ole Miss in 1962, but he thinks blacks must understand our history in order to plan for the future. Let us not forget that White America silenced Medgar Evers, Martin Luther King, Jr., Malcolm X, and Jimmie Lee Jackson [SCLC demonstrator killed in 1965 during a voter registration drive] just as Nada was silenced in the street in Tehran, Iran.

The dawn of summer was hotter that July; SCLC marchers yelled in the streets, "Down with dope, up with hope… tear down the crack houses…educate our children. SCLC's spokesman, Rev. Byron Clay, wanted the Mississippi State legislature to hear him. James Meredith wanted the Southern Baptist to hear his message. Was anybody listening?

Be patient when starting a new business

Rome wasn't built over night – it grew over years of toil and so will a new business.

By Meredith C. McGee, Jackson Advocate, Contributing Writer

During the early stages of a business, entrepreneurs can expect to experience an unsteady flow of revenue. They may have a steady stream of customers or business one week and have no cash inflow the following week. New business owners must have patience, because building a business takes time – years.

Business enjoyment is an added plus, since new business owners figuratively speaking *work their fingers right down to the bones* before an ounce of money is earned. Planning, hardwork, and the willingness to learn diverse business issues are critical to new business owners. Proprietors who toil through the hurdles may one day *smell the roses*.

Perspective new business entrepreneurs should be aware that until their business breaks even they will not start earning a profit and as George Rodriquez (2004), a Power Homebiz staff writer said, profit is the paycheck for a business owner. Rodriquez pointed out that the breakeven point shows what level of sales is needed to offset all the fixed costs (constant cost totals such as rent) and the variable costs (irregular cost totals like utilities) of producing products. When the business breaks even, expenses equal revenue, but *profit is zero*.

Studies have shown that it takes an average of three to five years for a business to breakeven. Rodriguez warned business start-up owners to make sure they have enough capital to cover expenses during this phase. Rodriquez said there are three indicators of a successful business.

1. Achieving the break-even point
2. Earning a living wage
3. Achieving real profit

The second stage of business success is earning a living wage, which Rodriquez said is similar to living from one pay check to another. When the business is achieving a real profit, it is earning discretionary (free cash which is unattached to living expenses) cash and earning a respectable wage," Rodriquez replied.

Starting a business exposes business owners to financial risks. Monetarily speaking, a new business can have a very negative impact on the family's budget, slicing entertainment and other liberal spending habits. Furthermore, some start-ups take great risks by using real estate and other assets as collateral for loan funds. The good news is planning and preparation can greatly reduce the risks associated with starting a business.

One of the BIG questions that perspective entrepreneurs need to discover is who will buy their product or use their service?

Let's take a look at a scenario about a good cook named Sarah. Sarah is a diabetic who developed a sugar-free pound cake that is light and tastes like it has real sugar in it. Sarah's family and friends are excited about her sugar free cake and they contend that the cake is a good business idea. However, Sarah may have a good business idea if consumers, like her family and friends, become excited about her product.

Paulette Thomas (2004), a writer for the Wall Street Journal's Center for Entrepreneurs, advises people interested in starting a business to, "define their market – by sales, demographic, region, or whatever applies. She added, "For start-ups information is power." So, Sarah should begin gathering market information. In addition, Sarah has invented a recipe that she may want to protect through U.S. copyright laws. The Library of Congress copyright division can be assessed on-line at www.copyright.gov or by calling (202)707-3000.

The U.S. Small Business Administration (2004) defines market research as, “the systematic and objective approach to gathering marketing information which – when processed, analyzed, and interpreted – will help identify problems and opportunities that allow for better-informed, lower-risk decisions.”

Let’s look at Sarah’s scenario again. Imagine that she conducted market research by getting 500 grocery store customers from 16 locations to taste a sample of her cake one Saturday morning. As a result, 180 of the customers marked on Sarah’s post card that they loved the cake and would purchase it if it was available. One hundred cake samplers reported that they were dieters, 60 were diabetic, 13 noted that they would purchase the cake on special occasions, and 7 people did not respond.

Henry Thomas, Director of JSU Small Business Development Center (SBDC), said Sarah’s scenario failed to ask an important question regarding the price a potential consumer would be willing to pay for the cake.” Henry Thomas remarked that it would be relevant to know how many people would purchase the cake for example $5 as opposed to a different price.

Larry Ward, a SBDC Business Counselor, says that although the market information showed that roughly a quarter of those polled had an interest in purchasing the sugar free cake, Sarah should proceed with caution and that her information questions should have asked those who sampled the cake to provide their age and gender. It would also be in Sarah’s best interest to obtain a business and marketing plan. The plan would show the break-even analysis for her business which would show her how many cakes must be sold before her business breaks even.

Henry Thomas suggested that a business plan is one of the most critical tools a perspective business owner can develop. Thomas stated, “You plan your work then work your plan.” He proclaimed that an entrepreneur should find out the particulars (age, buying habits) concerning the kinds of people included in a market segment (baby boomers, teens, professionals, etc.) to be able to reach their target market.

Although market analysis is an important aspect of business planning, company ownership, location, product and service information, management, personnel issues, financial projections, among other things are relevant planning topics. The résumés of key staff, leases, property deeds, company brochures, price lists, and statistics are often attached to business plans.

Angela Carson, President, Carson Consulting Services, prepares business plans for clients. Carson stated that individuals should realize that business plans are not just vehicles to obtain loan funds, but are designed to serve as comprehensive planning and marketing tools."

The U.S. Small Business Administration (SBA) offers a series of free on-line courses for start-up and growing businesses. The courses can be accessed at www.sba/gov/training/courses.html. Courses include How to Start a Business, Identifying the Target Market, Growth Strategies, Accounting and Finance, Is Franchising for Me?, A Primer on Exporting, Employee Handbook, Small Business Tax Workshops, and dozens of other topics. Sample business plans can also be downloaded from SBA's website.

Other Resources available to businesses are included in the chart below.

Firstgov.gov www.firstgov.gov/Business/Business_Gateway.shtml	Businesslaw.gov www.businesslaw.gov
Assn. of Small Business Development Centers www.asbdc-us.org (703) 764-9850	National Assn. for the Self-Employed www.nase.org (800) 232-6273

Henry Thomas reported that the SBDC, located in the JSU E-Center on Raymond Rd. (Old Allstate Building), offers one-on-

one counseling, technical assistance, business plan development, and other assistance all of which are confidential and free.

People interesting in obtaining a course schedule may call (601) 979-2795. Courtney Dudley, a perspective day care business owner, is utilizing the services. Dudley said she is being counseled which is providing her with the direction she needs to get her business off the ground.

Tim C. Lee, the owner of TCL Financial & Tax Service, recommended that “People should start home-based businesses before they obtain commercial leases.” While working for a tax service firm, Lee moonlighted and prepared taxes at home for clients. Henry Thomas pointed out that some new business owners (retail stores, entertainment enterprises, etc.) cannot conduct business from their homes, but he agreed that starting at home is a great way to cut expenses.

Lee stressed that a new business needs clients. Lee maintained that firms need clients and cash flowing in to pay the rent, phone bill, payroll, and other expenses. Lee added that people should keep their full-time jobs while building a client base. Flyers, business cards, advertisements, and word-of-month are a few methods that can assist proprietors to obtain clients.

The final take is that new proprietors should learn their potential market environment including their competitor’s pricing strategies as well as their potential industry’s product or service standards. A good business and marketing plan can provide a structured roadmap for any business owner.

Career Advice - Strong Cover Letters - Marketable Résumés and - The Interview

By Meredith C. McGee, Jackson Advocate, Contributing Writer

Job seekers, who are competing in today's job markets, will increase their chances of landing a job by fine-tuning their résumés, selling their skills through cover letters, and by utilizing good interviewing skills.

A study conducted by Accountemps found that 60% of executives believe the cover letter is as important as or more critical than a résumé. Yes, it is definitely unprofessional to send a résumé to a perspective employer without a cover letter. Cover letters should be attached even if one is submitting an electronic résumé.

The cover letter is a job seeker's chance to impress a perspective employee. The cover letter can explain why one is interested in a job and allows one to elaborate on his or her experience and career accomplishments.

Résumés that don't accent a job seekers experience or accomplishments or that are not producing any interviews typically need makeovers. Please note that one's age, sex, religious affiliation, and marital status have no reason to be on a résumé.

Job seekers, who graduated from college four of five years ago will want to transfer their entry level résumé into a more career oriented resume. At this point in one's career, it is more important to highlight the experience (on-the-job trainings, career achievements, etc) one has gained since graduating from college than it is to highlight the societies and clubs one belonged to during college.

When preparing a cover letter, remember to address the cover letter to a specific person such as someone in charge of hiring or a human resource manager. Make your objective fit each job application. The objective can be as specific as “Radiology Aide, Bookkeeping” or as broad as “Seeking a Licensed Practical Nurse position in a Pediatric Unit.”

Those with good spelling and writing skills should be able to prepare a winning cover letter and a professional résumé themselves. Résumé books are very resourceful for job seekers to follow when revising or preparing a résumé. At an average cost of $25, they offer hundreds of sample cover letters and résumés and provide information concerning capitalization, etc.

Unlike books, résumé templates found on most word processing programs provide a few samples cover letters and résumés and offer no information on the *nuts and bolts* of résumé writing. In addition, websites www.vault.com, www.CareerJournal.com, www.job-interview.net, www.jobsontheweb.com, provide career information.

As a rule, résumés and cover letters should be error free. People who lack the necessary technical skills needed to draft good quality cover letters and résumés should seek professional help.

If necessary, contact a professional résumé writer. There are at least eight services listed in the Yellow Pages under Resume Service. A number of printing companies also prepare résumés. The costs of résumé revisions range from $65 to $225. Price is irrelevant if the service can assist a job seeker to make the interview and job cut which after all is the ultimate goal of a job hunter.

A professional résumé writer can assist a person to smooth over employment gaps and provide career guidance. Some services offer employment testing and screening, mock interviews, and job search assistance. If you use a résumé service, make sure you obtain a copy of the résumé and cover letter on disk for future use.

Having an easy-to-read and well-designed résumé is essential to make the interview cut. According to CareerJournal.com, professionals responsible for screening your résumé will toss it to the side for any of the following reasons.

1. Your objective does not match the current opening.
2. Inappropriate or insufficient educational credential.
3. Incompatible salary requirements.
4. Poorly organized, sloppy, or hard-to-read (crowded) content.
5. Geographic restrictions incompatible with current opening.
6. A long list of employers in a short period of time.
7. Too much information.

Your professional résumé may land you an interview, but good interviewing skills will land you a job. Below are some interview tips to remember.

- Wear two piece suits and or solid colors. Avoid red and loud colors.
- Men should not wear earrings or braids.
- Neither sex should wear nose, face, or tongue rings.
- Women should wear one pair of earrings and limit jewelry. Jewelry may be *fashion fabulous*, but it is not fashionable during the career search.
- Never say anything negative about former employers or co-workers.
- Practice answering sample interview questions (What are your short term career goals? Why do you want to work for our company?).
- Arrive fifteen minutes early.
- Sit straight in your chair and remain calm.
- Provide a reasonable amount of eye contact.
- Take several copies of your résumé with you. You will want to review it and you may decide to leave another copy with the interviewer.

- Express long term interest in the company.
- If there is more than one interviewer, focus attention on each person.
- Read the company brochure and view the website before the interview.
- Give the interviewer a firm hand shake and thank him or her before leaving.
- Send the interviewer(s) a thank you note or card the following day.

When you are seeking a job, have a sound cover letter and a neatly formatted and well written résumé. Above all, be prepared for the interview. *Dress for success,* give the interviewer a firm hand shake, and don't forget to thank him or her for taking the time to interview you.

Lastly, obtain the interviewer's business card or contact information and send a thank you note or card the following day. Business etiquette (simple manners) can help someone make the *job cut*.

How Can African Americans Compete in Today's Job Market?

By Meredith C. McGee, Jackson Advocate, Contributing Writer

The old Negro adage "*First fired, last hired*" still applies to African Americans today. Whites, Hispanics, Asians, and others all obtain jobs faster than African Americans. The unemployment rate for African Americans historically has been higher than White Americans and this trend continues.

The U.S. Department of Labor reported that, there were 8.2 million persons reportedly unemployed in May of 2004. The African American community was hit the hardest during the past year with unemployment rates that were double and in some instances triple the rates of other nationalities.

In addition, the national unemployment rate for the month of April and May of 2004 was 5.6%. In contrast, the unemployment rate for African Americans was 10.2% in March and 9.7% in April, which was almost double the national average.

Basically, African Americans with skills are getting today's jobs and African American high school dropouts are the *last hired.* William Darity, an economics professor at the University of NC at Chapel Hill says, "The gap between better-educated blacks and less-educated blacks is wider than it was 20 years ago."

The trends are clear; it is easier for a white high school dropout to get a job today than it is for an African America dropout. Bernard Anderson, University of Pennsylvania's Wharton School adds that because of the wide gap between less-educated and college educated blacks, "it's committing labor suicide for an African American not to obtain an education, because his or her chance of obtaining a job is six times less than it would be with a degree." The employment levels for African Americans with college degrees was 3.3% in April compared to 2.3% for high school graduates. The unemployment rate was 12.8% for African American high school dropouts. However, in April the unemployment rate for whites with college degrees was 2.7%, the rate for high school graduates was 4.6%, and the rate for high school dropouts was 7.4%.

The U.S. Department of Labor reported that young women continue to attend college at higher rates than young men while African Americans continue to have low college enrollment rates. As of October 2003, Asians who graduated from high school last year had the highest college enrollment – 84.1%. The college enrollment for white graduates was 65% and the rate for Black and Hispanic graduates was 58%.

Last October, the unemployment rate for high school students was 16.1%; the rate for blacks was 33.2% and Hispanics was 22.7%. In contrast, the rate for white high school students was 12.8%.

African American college student's unemployment rate was 12.8%, which was double the rate of white college students (5.7%). Hispanic and Asian college student's rates were 6.8% and 6.6% respectively.

Youth who have less than a high school diploma also had high unemployment rates. They were 18.3% for men and 24.8% for women.

Many old economy jobs which require little or no skills such as those in the manufacture industry have closed shop and basically moved abroad where labor is cheap. New economy jobs require job seekers to have specialized training.

African Americans who lack specializations should seriously consider obtaining skills such as painting, plumbing, physical therapy, medical coding, etc. in order to compete in the job market.

It is a good idea to study job trends before pursuing advanced educations at trade schools or colleges. Some trades or degrees offer great potential job opportunities while others do not.

Obtaining skills can reduce the great odds that African Americans face of being shut out of the job market. For those who may be interested in relocating, the list below shows Ten American Cities with the lowest unemployment rates.

Rank	**City or Metropolitan Area**	**Unemployment Rate**	**Previous**
1	Bryan-College Station, TX	1.7%	1
2	Columbia, MO	1.9%	2
3	Charlottesville, VA	2.1	6
4 (tie)	Athens, GA	2.3%	3
4 (tie)	Gainesville, FL	2.3%	4
4 (tie)	Fort Walton Beach, FL	2.3%	8 (tie)
4 (tie)	Fargo, N.D. Moorehead, MN	2.3%	8 (tie)
4 (tie)	Bismarck, N.D.	2.3%	8 (tie)
9 (tie)	Enid, OK	2.5%	8 (tie)
9 (tie)	Madison, WI	2.5%	8 (tie)

Source: U.S. Labor Department March 2004

Where are the Hot Jobs?

People with skills are finding work today even though the economy is experiencing a recession. New jobs are available for hospital staff, teachers, managers, technical consultants, web designers, ultrasound technicians, physical therapists, office administrators, realtors, Wall Street brokers, and security specialists.

What is the pay ranges for various jobs in the Jackson Metropolitan area?

A chef in the tri-county Jackson, MS Metropolitan area earns an average of $47,000 per year. The lowest pay for a chef is $31,000 and the highest pay is $114,000. The chart below shows the wages of other jobs in the area. The numbers have been rounded up.

Job Position	**Average Annual Wages**	**Lowest Rate of Pay**	**Highest Rate of Pay**
Chemist	$40,000	$29,000	$49,000
Computer System Analyst	$46,000	$35,000	$63,000
Customer Service Manager	$56,000	$43,000	$72,000
Physical Therapist	$63,000	$45,000	$74,000
Electric Engineer	$51,000	$39,000	$62,000
Urban Planner	$36,000	$25,000	$42,000
University President	$58,000	$39,000	$71,000
Purchase Agent	$39,000	$28,000	$49,000
Public Accountant	$51,000	$36,000	$71,000
Webmaster	$57,000	$43,000	$74,000

Source: CareerJournal.com

African American job seekers can become more marketable by obtaining specialized skills and trades. The medical, teaching, real estate and other fields are expected to have job growth in the future. Many local college and universities offer advance educational opportunities that take from two to five years to complete.

The Career Development Center offer trades or areas of specialization such as word processing and refrigeration maintenance. The center's phone number is 601-960-5322.

Job Corps of American in Crystal Springs, MS offers a variety of trades from plumbing to business office technology for youth who are at least sixteen years old. Job Corps also accepts high school dropouts. Job Corps phone number is 601-948-6443.

A skilled labor force is needed in the new economy. African Americans who have not completed high school or who lack skills are more likely than any other race to end up standing in the unemployment line.

James Howard Meredith: A living legend

Biography: James Howard Meredith
Lecturer, Entrepreneur, Author, Second Reconstruction Pioneer
Born: June 25, 1933
Birthplace: Kosciusko, Attala County, Mississippi

Not so long ago, in 1962, during a time when racial strife was as thick as thieves or rather bandits, James Howard Meredith integrated the University of Mississippi which had been chartered as Mississippi's first public university in 1848. Mr. Meredith's deed gave blacks hope and put a bitter taste in the mouth of white segregationists. Though victory was nowhere in sight educational opportunities once closed tight to Colored citizens were opened.

The media described Mr. Meredith's action as brave, daring, and nutty. Because he was bold enough to risk his life to force America to make a "lily white" university honor his right under the law to obtain an education at its institution, people were baffled by him and many misunderstood him.

After his father passed, James Meredith did things his way and by standards established by himself. His father had taught him to think for himself, to do what he thought was right, and had believed he would make good choices.

Besides his father, James Meredith admired biblical characters: Moses, David, and Jesus. Historically, he was taken by General Napoleon Bonaparte who had conquered the world before he was 30 years old. Meredith was himself 29 years old when he became a champion for his race.

At age 73 James Meredith had arrived and become monumental worthy, an honor normally reserved for the deceased. The very school that closed the door to him and his kind up until September 30, 1962 erected a Civil Rights Monument and a 6'2 life size statute in his honor which was unveiled October 1, 2006, 44 years after he attended his first day of class.

As the Statute Unveiling program unfolded, James Meredith sat on the podium next to his pretty wife, Judy, in a tailored white suit with a black and white bowtie as cool as he had been when he walked across the campus for the first time in 1962 escorted by U.S. Marshals. In 2006, his thick, manicured, black and white beard gave him a distinguished look, and he is just that – one of a kind. James Meredith is his own man in his own right.

James Meredith started off in life the middle child of a black farmer. He grew up on an 84-acre farm four and a half miles outside of Kosciusko, Mississippi in Attala County which is located in central Mississippi, a southern American state. He was his father's seventh child and his mother's first born. His parents Moses Arthur "Cap" Meredith and Roxie Mariah Patterson married April 4, 1931.

Cap and Roxie named James Meredith the initials - J.H. when he was born. Like his older siblings, J.H. called his father Cap and his mother Ms. Roxie. J.H. was affectionately called J-Boy by his family and friends. Three years before J.H. was born, the parents in his rural community pooled their resources together and founded Cook Private School. Cap and the black investors used cows, horses, and other items as collateral to secure a loan with Merchants & Farmers Bank to finance the school. In those days, blacks had to create their own institutions, because the white power structure did not appropriate sufficient funds to create schools, hospitals, and other institutions to benefit blacks.

When J-Boy was three years old, he starting walking to Cook Private School which was near their farm with his sisters Thelma and Miriam who were age 12 and 10 respectively. His oldest brother, Emmett, became the first high school graduate in the family that year, and his older siblings Leroy and Delma were attending high school at Attala County Training School in Kosciusko.

Graduating from high school was rare for southern blacks in 1935-36; in fact, at that time, over 170,000 out of one million Mississippi blacks were illiterate. When J-Boy was four years old, he learned to say his ABCs forward and backward. Early in life he was challenged to keep up with his older sisters and brothers which caused him to develop a burning desire to learn and to achieve. J-Boy's parents and older brothers and sisters encouraged his educational progress, and he excelled academically.

Although Cap had a fifth-grade education, he understood that an education was connected to one's income and quality of life. He missed the opportunity to obtain a job that paid good wages because he did not have an eighth-grade education. Roxie had obtained an eighth-grade education in a one room school called The Patterson School which had been created by her father, William Patterson, and other members of the Center Community in the early 1900s. The school went to the eighth grade, but there was no high school in that section of the county.

J-Boy was mixed with African, Indian, and White blood. The Patterson lineage included an Irish immigrant, who arrived in South Carolina in the early 1800s. His Mulatto slave, Caroline, was moved to Center, Mississippi. Ned Meredith, J-Boy's paternal grandfather, was a sharecropper for four decades. His entire family including his children worked in the fields. He obtained a railroad job later in life.

Cap's mother Francis Brown Meredith was Ned's second wife. Francis, the illegitimate daughter of a white lawyer, JAP Campbell, was a school teacher, but after her marriage she was not allowed to keep her position. She secretly taught her nine children reading, writing, and math on rainy days and during the evenings. Ned's oldest son, James Cleveland (J.C.), grew up in

Ned and Francis' home; unlike Francis, Ned and J.C. were both illiterate.

Cap was a natural leader and the name "Cap" was derivative of the word captain. He was an expert farmer, who had learned many farming techniques on The Hamilton Farm in Holmes County, Mississippi. While serving as a sharecropper on a white man's farm in 1923, Cap offered some planting advice to the land owner, who rejected his suggestions. The land owner said, "Now, Cap if you want to boss you need to go and buy your own land."

The next day, Cap searched for some farm land and thereafter he purchased an 84-acre plot of land. The farm included a farm house and Cap, his first wife Barbara, and their four children immediately moved into the house in April of 1923. Ownership of land gave the family the freedom to allow their children to receive a better quality of education in comparison to the substandard education available to sharecroppers. A week shy of Christmas in 1929, Barbara passed away while undergoing a gallbladder surgery in Jackson. Her passing was a difficult experience for the family.

Roxie moved on the farm several years after Barbara's passing. During J-Boy's young life, Roxie was a housewife; she provided educational support to her children at home, and made it her personal business to attend all of their school programs. J-Boy learned a lot from his five older siblings who were seven to 17 years older than him.

By the time J-Boy was seven years old, four of his older siblings had left home. By 1943, Miriam was the oldest child at home and J-Boy became the oldest boy on the farm. He provided leadership to his three younger siblings, and taught them how to take care of the crops and animals.

On a few occasions, J-Boy accompanied his parents to the doctor's office in Kosciusko. On one visit, he noticed that his father's doctor had obtained a degree from the University of Mississippi (Ole Miss). J-Boy developed a desire to attend "Ole Miss" long before he realized Jim Crow laws would not allow him to attend an all-white college. His two older sisters Delma and Thelma obtained a teaching certificate from Rust College and Miriam enrolled in Jackson College for Negro Teachers, now called Jackson State University, after completing high school. J-Boy's youngest sister Willie Lou was born in 1947; when she turned three years old, he left home.

When J-Boy was a toddler, his oldest brother Emmett moved to St. Petersburg, Florida to stay with his uncle Cliff and his sister Miriam moved to Florida in 1949. Cliff was Cap's youngest brother, who never married and did not have any children. He was a security guard, and he had a roomy house in one of the most beautiful cities in America. J-Boy had learned that living with uncle Cliff was quite an adventure. When J-Boy completed the 11th grade his father sent him to live with his uncle Cliff to finish his 12th grade year.

During the summer, after completing the 11th grade, J-Boy moved to St. Petersburg and his uncle Cliff enrolled him in Gibbs High School as a senior. The school was much better than the schools J-Boy attended in Mississippi because the teachers had obtained bachelors and masters degrees, and the school curriculum was more advanced.

While in Florida, J.H. renamed himself James Howard Meredith in order to obtain a Florida Driver's license because the clerk would not accept the initials J.H. as an official name. His name choice was easily accomplished because his cousin J.C., who previously enlisted in the military had renamed himself James Cleveland Meredith, after his grandfather.

That school year, J-Boy submitted an essay entry to his teacher so she could enter his paper into the American Legion Essay Contest. After reviewing his paper, his teacher reasoned that the paper was poorly written and she rewrote his paper and asked him to sign off on the new paper. The new paper was entitled, *Why J.H. is Proud to be an American.* However, J.H. refused to acknowledge the paper his teacher had written. So, he rewrote his paper and sent his entry directly to the contest officials himself. The teacher was not happy that J.H. did not cooperate with her and she tried to get his entry disqualified, but the contest officials accepted his submission. In reality, his original essay was opposed because his theme had discussed how America could become a better place, and his teacher was not comfortable with the idea of her student challenging white customs.

J.H. won 1st place in the contest, and two white girls won 2nd and 3rd place. Their pictures made front page in the *St. Petersburg Times* newspaper. However, J.H. was not supported by school officials. The principal of the school publicly criticized J.H. as the contest winner, claiming he did not speak correct English.

In spite of the controversy surrounding the contest, J.H. graduated from high school in 1951. Like his older brother, Leroy, he enlisted in the Air Force. J.H., whose official name was James in the Armed Serves, served in an integrated military unit and became a clerk typist. He used his military benefits to attend college. While stationed in Indiana, James met and fell in love with Mary June Wiggins and the couple got married in 1956 in Gary, Indiana.

The military gave James a steady income and at age 19, Cap encouraged James to make his first real estate investment. James took his father's advice and sent $400 home and Cap purchased 40 acres of land from his sister Alberta Meredith Estes for $10 per acre. Shortly afterward, Cap purchased 15 acres for James which included the original site of the Cook Private School which had become the Marble Rock Public School. In 1959, James completed payments to purchase his father's farm land so that his aging parents would have the money they needed to purchase a lot and build a house in Kosciusko on Allen Street. His parent's house was completed in 1960. James took good advice, started many business enterprises, and became a self-made businessman.

James and Mary June's first child, John was born at a U.S. Air Force base in Tachikawa Japan on January 19, 1960. That year, after nine years of service, James received an honorable discharge from the military and that spring he relocated his family to Jackson, Mississippi. They moved into Maple Street Apartments which was near Lanier High School and enrolled in Jackson State College (now Jackson State University). Mississippi was a different world from Japan; in Japan, a black man was an American. In Mississippi, black men were being lynched, beaten, and terrorized for attempting to exercise their constitutional rights.

President John F. Kennedy was inaugurated into office on January 20, 1961, and James decided to try to accomplish one of his childhood dreams. That day, he wrote a letter draft and he mailed the letter the following day as an initial step to apply to attend Ole Miss. Shortly thereafter, James' application was acknowledged by the school's registrar. Robert Ellis thanked James for his application and informed him that the application process required a picture attachment, and three letters of reference to be furnished by school alumni. The photograph was required to reveal an applicant's race. The discriminatory photograph practice had been banned in the military during President Harry Truman's administration for over a decade, but the practice was alive and well in the south.

James Meredith did not know any white person who would write a letter on his behalf. In the 1960s, whites followed the Jim Crow rules which separated the races and rendered blacks second class citizens. Mississippi white citizens and elected officials opposed the 1954 Supreme Court ruling in the *Brown v. School Board* case which had called for the immediate integration of America's segregated school systems.

James wrote the registrar's office and informed the school that he was an American Negro citizen. The following letter from the school informed James that his application to attend the University of Mississippi was denied because the school could not accept the college credits he had acquired while he was in the military. However, Jackson State College was run by the same College Board, and it had accepted James' college credits, and he had enrolled as a junior. In reality, school officials did not want him to attend "Ole Miss" because he was black.

James had befriended Medgar Wiley Evers, who was a community activist that worked for the National Association for the Advancement of Colored People (NAACP). Evers had unsuccessfully attempted to seek admission to "Ole Miss" himself in 1954 and was very familiar with the enrollment process. Mr. Evers coached James and advised him to seek the assistance of the NAACP's Legal Defense Fund, which was led by Thurgood Marshall. The Legal Defense Fund agreed to utilize their paid council to assist James with his legal needs. Marshall had served as the lead attorney for the *Brown v. School Board* case, and he later became the first black Supreme Court justice.

Thurgood Marshall appointed Constance Motley, an attorney from New York to serve on James Meredith's case. She was a well-known civil rights attorney, who had served on many school desegregation cases. R. Jesse Brown, a local black civil rights attorney joined James Meredith's defense team too; case documents were filed in the courts under Attorney Brown's Mississippi license.

At that time Brown was one of four black attorneys in the state of Mississippi. Brown filed the first civil rights lawsuit in Mississippi. Prior to serving on Meredith's legal team, one of Brown's black client's Mack Charles Parker was abducted from jail by a mob in 1959, lynched, and thrown in the Pearl River before his trial began. With their lives and their client's life at risk, for nearly two years, the attorneys worked diligently to assist Meredith with his integration lawsuit.

After winning the right to attend the all-white college by the Fifth Circuit Court of Appeals, James Meredith was blocked from enrolling in the school by Governor Ross Barnett at the Woolfolk Building in Jackson. On another occasion, the governor refused to allow James to complete his registration on campus. The Lieutenant Governor, Paul Johnson, and a group of white men formed a solid line and blocked James and the U.S. Marshal's path to the administration office on James third registration attempt.

The Fifth Circuit Court of Appeals imposed a $10.000 fine on Governor Barnett and a $5,000 fine on Lieutenant Governor Johnson per day until they ceased interfering with the registration of James Meredith to the University of Mississippi. The fine impressed upon the governor and the lieutenant governor to cease their personal interference with James Meredith's registration process. After the state leaders directly stepped aside, white citizens collaborated with the Klu Klux Klan and organized groups to oppose James Meredith's registration.

Shortly thereafter, Ole Miss had a football game and Governor Ross Barnett incited the crowd. "Never, Never!" they screamed. The governor said, "Never shall our emblem go, from Colonel "Reb" to Old Black Joe!" The governor was implying to whites that they would never have to worry about giving up their customs of separating the races. The Never doctrine, popularized by the governor, turned into a protest movement, and students started wearing Never pins attached to their clothing.

However, President John F. Kennedy ordered the involvement of the U.S. Marshals Service and the tides quickly changed. On September 30, 1962, James Meredith, who was protected by several U.S. Marshals, spent the night in Baxter Hall on the school's campus. James was finally scheduled to complete his registration the following morning with the support of the U.S. Marshals Service which had been sent on campus by President John. F. Kennedy and Attorney General Robert Kennedy.

News of James Meredith's arrival angered white racists and thousands started descending on the school's campus from Alabama, Georgia, Louisiana, Mississippi, and Texas earlier that Sunday morning. That night a riot broke out between private white citizens and U.S. Marshals and the National Guard. The riot escalated into an insurrection and resulted in the injuries of 168 marshals and 200 soldiers. Twenty-nine people received shotgun wounds; at least six people received acid burns, and two whites were killed on campus.

The following morning, James was driven to the administration building to complete his registration. The car used to drive him to the building reflected the aftermath of the insurrection. It was riddled with bullet holes and the glass was broken out. However, James Meredith registered for classes October 1, 1962; he attended his first class, Colonial American History.

The white students were not friendly to him. He became the most unpopular student on campus. Even though, James was escorted around campus by U.S. Marshals the entire school semester, some students threw fire crackers at him and cursed him. Some of them simply hated him because the color of his skin was too dark for their liking. A few students believed blacks had the right to attend school with them, but most were afraid to break their silence, and the few who did were persecuted.

James ignored the student's derogatory remarks. He considered himself a soldier fighting a battle for him and his kind. He felt he had won a battle when he completed his registration and joined the student population of the best college in the state of Mississippi. Now other blacks could follow in his footsteps. James Meredith became an important part of history when he integrated Ole Miss. Prior to that point, black students had to move outside of the state of Mississippi to attend law school and medical school because there were no law schools or medical schools in Mississippi for black students to attend.

James obtained a Bachelor of Art degree in Political Science, History, and French. He walked across the stage and became the first black student to graduate from Ole Miss August 18, 1963. To taunt his classmates, James wore a Never button upside down on his suit jacket as he walked to the line-up area when they were preparing to walk across the stage in the graduation ceremony. James Meredith risked his life to break down Mississippi's segregation policies. Since 1962, many black Mississippians have become lawyers, medical doctors, pharmacists, veterinarians, and entered other professions.

After graduation, James and his family moved to Nigeria and he enrolled in Ibadan University and obtained a Masters degree in Government and Economics in 1965. Immediately afterward they moved to New York City. While in New York, Mary June became a school teacher, and he enrolled in law school, and started writing *Three Years in Mississippi* which was published in 1966. The book discussed his college days at Jackson State College, and the legal battles which were pursued so he could integrate Ole Miss.

James Meredith returned to his home state from New York and started *The Walk Against Fear* in June of 1966. However, the walk was aborted on the second day (June 6, 1966) when he was shot in Hernando, Mississippi by a sniper. Martin Luther King Jr., Stokely Carmichael, and other civil rights leaders continued the walk. The walk was renamed the *Meredith March Against Fear* in honor of James Meredith. Under the direction of various civil rights leaders, thousands of people joined the march and walked from the site of the shooting in Hernando, Mississippi on Highway 51 to Jackson, Mississippi.

James had organized the walk in hopes of influencing blacks to set aside their fear of the white power structure, and to encourage black voter registration. In general blacks continued to fear the white power structure, but over 5,000 blacks registered to vote during the walk that became a march. Although, the walk gave the participants a sense of accomplishment, there were not enough black registered voters in Mississippi for them to elect many candidates of their choice. James returned to New York afterward and he completed law school at Columbia University in 1968. Later that year, James Meredith walked 1,000 miles from Chicago to New York to underscore the DeFactor segregation and discrimination in the North.

Afterward, he attended Merrill Lynch Securities and Investment School and entered an internship as a stock broker for a short time. He returned to Mississippi in the 1970s, and created several business enterprises to supplement his tree farming operations. He operated a magazine called, *Outlook Magazine,* and one of the popular entertainment businesses he owned was called Chimneyville. The magazine regularly published the monthly arrests records of private citizens residing in Jackson, Mississippi. The DUI, burglary, prostitution, and other records embarrassed the accused and their family, but the articles were informative.

James Meredith used his voice to discuss political and social issues. A 1976 headline blasted the Jackson Police Department for filing trumped up charges against a black 16 year old teenage male. The October 1983 Issue, printed an interview with Charles Evers, brother of slain Civil Rights leader Medgar W. Evers. Charles Evers had become the first black Mayor of Fayette, Mississippi in 1968, and ran as an Independent for Governor of Mississippi. James Meredith and Charles Evers had one thing in common, they both opposed liberal political views and eventually become among a few from their era to join the Republican Party. Today, Mr. Meredith does not publicly discuss his political views, and though he ran for public office a few times he was never elected.

Mary June unexpectedly passed from heart failure in 1979. James and his three sons, John, Joseph, and James were devastated by her passing. As hard as it was, they picked up the pieces and continued to live their lives. Shortly afterward, James founded the African Development and Reunification Association. The purpose of the organization was to reunify all black people in the world. The organization's vision was never accomplished. The following year he married his second wife, Judy Alsobrooks, a Gary, Indiana school teacher.

During the late 1980s, James relocated his family to Cincinnati, Ohio. Judy started working at a local television station as a news reporter and James starting teaching African American Studies at the University of Cincinnati. James Meredith conducted the research to write his volume of 11 books at the Library of Congress while employed by Senator Jesse Helms from 1989-1991.

In 1995 James Meredith published a volume of 11 books. James wanted to obtain a position in Washington so that he could have access to the Library of Congress which is the largest library in the U.S. He had applied for a position with all 435 members of congress. Jesse Helms was one of two congressmen to respond to James job request letter. In 1997, he founded The Meredith Institute, started promoting the 3 Rs (reading, writing, arithmetic), advocating that blacks should learn proper English, and that males can become intellectual giants by mastering the English language.

James Meredith completed a book entitled *A Mission From God: A Memoir and Challenge for America* with historian and author William Doyle through Simon & Schuster in August of 2012 on the eve of the 50th Anniversary of Meredith's integration of Ole Miss. The book discussed Meredith's encounters with Martin Luther King, Jr., Robert J. Kennedy, Mary McCloud, Governor Ross Barnett, Thurgood Marshall, David Duke, and Medgar Evers. The memoir provides a manifesto for a better world.

A biography entitled *James Meredith: Warrior and the America that created him* written by his niece Meredith Coleman McGee was published by Praeger Publishing on March 21, 2013. It was classified as a textbook, and emerged as a Popular Culture/Ethnic Studies required reading. McGee's mother and Meredith's sister, Hazel Janell Meredith (Hazel Hall) published *My Brother J-Boy*, an illustrated children's book which describes their upbringing in rural Attala County, Mississippi in 2011. *A story about James H. Meredith – A Civil Rights Leader* by Dorothy Mays with Hazel Janell Meredith was written for beginning readers. Mays initiated the book project when she was an elementary school teacher in Memphis Public School system because there was no literature on James Meredith in the Memphis public school system.

Today there is a growing body of work on Mr. Meredith. Other book titles include: *An American Insurrection: James Meredith and the Battle of Oxford, Mississippi, 1962* by William Doyle; *James Meredith and the Ole Miss Riot: A Soldier's Story* by Gene Roberts and Henry T. Gallagher; *Price of Defiance: James Meredith and the Integration of Ole Miss* by Charles W. Eagles, and *The Battle of Ole Miss: Civil Rights v. States' Rights* by Frank Lambert.

Over the years, James Meredith has visited numerous countries to study the condition of people of color including Senegal, Guinea, Sierra Leone, Liberia, Togo, Benin, Nigeria, Egypt, Kenya, Tanzania, Zimbabwe, Zambia, Brazil, and France. Today, James and Judy Meredith live in Jackson, Mississippi. They are the proud parents of four surviving children and the grandparents of 12 grandchildren. Their son, Dr. Joseph Meredith passed from complications with Lupus in February of 2008. James continues to lecture to groups upon request. He gives audiences educational success tips and advocates that grandparents, parents, and guardians should prepare their children for pre-school at home.

James Meredith, Charles Evers, and Hollis Watkins, were key tour speakers for ACRES (American Civil Rights Education Services, Inc. which brought thousands of New York high school students to the South to learn Civil Rights history. Robert "Bob" Moses was a regular tour speaker until he moved from Jackson, Mississippi to Florida. ACRES participants were required to read Civil Rights history and met various leaders who presently live in the Deep South during a 10 day tour. The tours ended when ACRES founded Sean Devlin passed away 2006.

On May 25, 2012, at age 78, James Meredith launched his Walk for Education and Truth at the Tennessee/ Mississippi state line advocating that it takes a whole community to raise a child and challenging the church to take an active role in the lives of every child within a two mile radius of its doors by maintaining a record on each child. Parishioners of West Grove Church of Christ took a group photograph with James Meredith and Pastor Chuck Meador, Senturian DuReaux, and Fred Watson during the walk at the site where Meredith had been shot in Hernando, Mississippi in 1966.

The 40th Anniversary of the *Meredith Walk Against Fear* was organized by Jackson State University, and commemorated June 3, 2006 at the state Capitol in Jackson, Mississippi. Dr. Martin Luther King Jr., Stokely Carmichael, and others had ended the *Meredith March Against Fear* June 26, 1966 and spoke to a crowd of 30,000 onlookers at the state capitol.[1]

The *Meredith March Against Fear* was the last mass Civil Rights demonstration during the Second Reconstruction. Historians refer to the march as the end of the Civil Rights era, proposing that Stokely Carmichael launched the Black Power Movement when he introduced black power ideology during the *Meredith March Against Fear* in Greenwood, Mississippi.

[1] Lerone Bennett, Jr. "Before the Mayflower: A history of Black America." New York, NY: Penguin Books, 578.

The unveiling of a Civil Rights Memorial and a 6'2 statute of the hero was held at the University of Mississippi, October 1, 2006. The statute depicts James Meredith walking, and he has walked many miles in hopes of him and his kind obtaining equal citizenship rights and access to *The American Dream*.

James Meredith is a living legend, who has received numerous honors for his contribution to higher education and to the obtainment of equal citizenship rights for Americans. On May 29, 2013, he was the recipient of Harvard Graduate School of Education's Medal for Education Impact, the highest honor given by the school during the school's Convocation ceremony where he was a guest speaker. The following evening he had the pleasure of meeting Oprah Winfrey for the first time at a private dinner. She had also been a Convocation ceremony speaker at Harvard University. Both Meredith and Winfrey are Kosciusko's most famous citizens.

Today James Howard Meredith is fulfilling his speaking and book signing engagements. He exercises regularly, enjoys life, and continues to develop ways to use his voice for those who are lost in the shadows of a society plagued by classicism and discrimination.

By Meredith Coleman McGee

References

Bennett, Jr. L. (1988) *Before the Mayflower: A history of Black America*. New York, NY: Penguin Books.

Fleming, K. (2005). *Son of the rough south: Uncivil memoir*. Canada: Perseus Books Group. Meredith, J. (1966).

Meredith, J.H. *Three years in Mississippi*. Bloomington: Indiana University Press. Reprinted (1995). Jackson, MS: Meredith Publishing.

Meredith, J. (2000). James Meredith "A living legend." [Brochure]. Jackson, MS: The Meredith Institute.

Meredith, J. (1983, October). Who and what is Charles Evers? Outlook, 10(1), 1-13.

Meredith, M.C. (2013). *James Meredith: Warrior and the America that created him*. Santa Barbara, CA: Praeger Publishing.

The University of Mississippi. (2008). Ole Miss History. Retrieved March 26, 2008 from, http://www.olemiss.edu/info/history.html

Civil Rights icon's vision for the poor

"I ain't' dead yet," James Meredith proclaimed to a MS Delta woman. His remarks may be an indication that he has more work to do in the years ahead.

Over half a century ago, Thurgood Marshall, who headed the NAACP's Legal Defense Fund, did not expect Meredith to actually carry out plans to integrate the University of Mississippi. Marshall's doubt insulted Meredith, but perhaps Marshall was reminded that a college teacher, Clennon W. King, Jr., who appeared on campus at Ole Miss in 1958, was taken from the registration site, committed into an asylum, and driven out of the state. Meredith was described by author, William Doyle as a man ahead of his time for envisioning in 1960 that White Supremacy could be broken. Others have described him as eccentric, but some will not dispute that he is a man with a mission for the poor that is none other than timely.

Meredith's Walk for the Poor began in Tunica, MS, May 24, 2009 on Hwy 61 S., where 33 percent of the population and 40 percent of blacks live in poverty, among the highest rates in America. Since then, he has walked through areas of Senatobia, Sardis, Crenshaw, Marks, Clarksdale, Tutwiler, Drew, Ruleville, Mayersville, Belzoni, Vicksburg, Canton, and other towns. He walked in several wards in Greenwood accompanied by Councilman Charles McCoy. Meredith told an audience in Tutwiler Monday at the Tutwiler Community Education Center, "I've learned more in the past week about America than I've ever known. People are crying and some people have given up." Meredith said, "It makes me sad that the majority of children who graduate from the public school system do not achieve college entrance scores high enough to get accepted into state colleges, making this walk more important than Ole Miss." He proposed that America has the best public school system in Western Civilization, but children cannot take advantage of the system when they are not been prepared for school. He believes we will not lose another generation of children if parents, grandparents, and guardians teach their children the fundamentals before they go to school.

Meredith started passing out bookmarks in the MS Delta June, 1, 2009 which tells parents, grandparents, and guardians to teach their children their ABCs and how to count to 100 before age five and before they go to school. Hundreds of people have gotten their bookmarks autographed. He hopes the message of school preparedness will resonate with parents. "When Booker T. Washington was seven years old, he attended General Hampton's school. General Hampton[iii] sent Booker T. Washington to AL to start a school. My daddy and many others started schools from that example," Meredith proclaimed.

James H. Meredith rear of March Photo by Meredith C. McGee

"After slavery schools were in the churches. I attended a one room school. The eighth graders taught the sixth graders and the sixth graders taught the fourth graders," Meredith recalled. The church was once the pillow of the community. Meredith believes the Christian community is in a position to solve problems relating to the plight of the poor.

Thirty thousand people listened to Dr. Martin Luther King, Jr, Stokely Carmichael and others speak at the state capitol in Jackson, MS on June 26, 1966. This march was the last massage mobilization during the Second Reconstruction; participation was driven by NAACP, SCLC, SNCC, CORE, and the Urban League, and donations were provided to offset the cost of the events. Compared to four decades ago, low participation in SCLC's Poor Man's Campaign kick-off in Jackson, MS and Meredith's Walk for the Poor in 2009 in MS is revelation that few are willing to publicly protest the plight of the poor.

Meredith has a vision that when the church expands its missionary work for the poor in its community, when the Southern Baptist completes its unfinished missionary work to blacks, and when home is where children get their educational foundation, conditions of the poor will improve.

By Meredith C. McGee

Woman on a Lamar Street porch speaking to marchers

House on Lamar Street along the March route

SCLC Poor People's Campaign Photo by Meredith C. McGee

Church of Christ Holiness U.S.A. Lamar Street, Jackson, MS
Photo by Meredith C. McGee

Historically black university in Jackson, Miss. to present television programming to local area

By Meredith Coleman, Advocate Writer

Judy Alsobrooks[iv]*, general manager and principal developer of W23BC and Vincent Wright, production coordinator look forward to opening up JSU's television station.*

Soon Jacksonians can turn to channel 23 and see Jackson State University mass communication student reporters hosting a local news and two local talk shows on a new television outlet. The programming will cater to African American audiences. The low power television station, W23BC is scheduled to go on air by mid-summer.

"I'm enthusiastic that Jackson State, one of the top historically black universities will have television programming for the metropolitan Jackson area," stated Judy Alsobrooks, general manager and principal developer of W23BC. Overall Jackson State students and faculty share the same perspective.

Alsobrooks has been in the industry for more than a decade as a reporter, anchor, and most recently assignment editor of WAPT channel 16 here in Jackson, "We feel this is very exciting, not only for the students, but for the community as well," she explained.

"W23 will potentially serve 28,000 viewers within a 10 mile radius of the station. The viewership constitutes a 79 percent African American audience; the other 21 percent is white, Asian, Hispanic and Native American. The programming side will draw upon participation by local museums, schools, the Jackson Zoo and the audience within W23's viewer radius," Alsobrooks added. The television station is still in the developmental stages but Alsobrooks is optimistic that it will become a powerful educational tool and laboratory for JSU students as well as others.

"The students will be trained in all facets of the profession," said Alsobrooks. This training will add to student upward mobility in the job market since each student will leave the courses armed with a sample tape that will show potential employers what they can contribute. "This is invaluable for students because they will be entering a diverse and competitive market,' said Alsobrooks.

The expertise of other departments at JSU will be utilized for L.P.T.V. The Computer Modeling Laboratory in the Science Department will create needed graphics. Dale Morris of the Jackson State Music Department will compose sounds.

"The T.V. program will have the contemporary look similar to other local stations, if not more so," explained Alsobrooks. "We will have the available resources to put together professional graphics and other visual effects, along with substantial content. We'll also provide significant air time for community information; other stations can't dedicate the amount of air time. Periodical news briefs will also be featured.

Vincent Wright, production coordinator, says viewer needs and interests are generally speaking, not being met locally. Plans are being implemented at W23BC to fill a specific gap in the local news coverage with more educational, entertaining and informational programming.

"We want to educate the community by providing alternative viewpoints instead of providing issues onesidedly. We want to dig deeper into the state's wealth that generally goes untapped. We plan to show the positive aspects African Americans opposed to the trends of focusing on negative community programs. Further, we are in the midst of the origin of Jazz and Blues music. This part of our culture has not been given the reverence it deserves," Wright stated.

The two talk shows "Today's Black Women" and "Brother 2 Brother" will feature issues that relate to men and women.

Alternatives that will help keep the family unit together will be a primary focus. Programs will also focus on issues concerning the elderly, youth, and the growing Spanish and Indian communities," he added.

Wright's philosophy is that African Americans have the opportunity to become 'super powers.' "We have gotten the civil rights behind us, and the world is changing through technology. We can make a similar transformation to what the Japanese did after World War II. But we must prepare ourselves to take advantage of technology. When the old television goes out, buy the children a computer instead of replacing it," he argues.

Timeline for James Howard Meredith June 25, 1933 –

By Meredith Coleman McGee

James Meredith was born June 25, 1933 to Moses Arthur and Roxie Mariah Patterson Meredith. His given name was J.H. He was his father's seventh child and his mother's firstborn. Moses was known to all as "Cap."

J.H. grew up on the outskirts of Kosciusko, Mississippi on an 84-acre farm.

At age three, in 1936, he started school at Cook Private School. Cap and local black farmers used their cattle, and livestock as collateral to obtain a bank loan from Merchants and Farmers Bank in Kosciusko to finance the school.

J.H. was called J-Boy by his family and people in the community.

Attala County took over the school which had been established with private funds during the 1939-1940 school year, and Cap stepped down from the board, withdrew his children from Cook Private School, and enrolled them in Attala County Training School in Kosciusko.

J.H., a 1st grader walked 4 1/2 miles to school which took one hour. He completed the 11th grade at Attala County Training School.

Cap's youngest brother Cliff enrolled J.H. in Gibbs High School in St. Petersburg, Florida for his senior school year (1950-1951).

The clerk at the driver's license department in Florida, refused to issue J.H. a license with initials, so he changed his name from J.H. to James Howard.

He graduated from high school in 1951, and went to Detroit to enlist in the Air Force. Blacks couldn't enlist in the armed services in the south at that time.

James Meredith served in the Air Force from 1951-1960.

In 1956, James Meredith married Mary June Wiggins in Gary, Indiana.

He obtained an honorable discharge in 1960 and he and his wife, Mary June and their son, John Howard, who was born in Japan moved to Mississippi and the couple enrolled in Jackson State College.

JFK gave a Civil Rights platform speech during his campaign to win over black voters, and the day he took office Jan 21, 1960, James Meredith wrote a letter seeking admission to the University of Mississippi (Ole Miss).

A college friend introduced James Meredith to Medgar Wiley Evers, who became a key member of James Meredith's advisory team. Mr. Evers contacted Thurgood Marshal who headed the NAACP's Legal Defense Fund.

Marshal assigned Constance Motley from NY to work on James Meredith's legal case. R Jess Brown, who had a license to practice law in Mississippi joined the team too. Court documents where filed under Brown's license.

The legal team fought the case for nearly two years. They argued the case on the local level and lost, appealed to the 5th Court of Appeals, and went all the way to the Supreme Court.

After winning the right to attend Ole Miss, Governor Ross Barnett, the Lieutenant Governor, Paul B. Johnson blocked three of James Meredith's registration attempts.

The court imposed $10K and $5K fines on both men respectively to demand they cease their interference with the court order.

On September 30, 1960, JFK, RFK, and Governor Ross Barnett negotiated a plan to allow James Meredith to become a resident on the Campus of Ole Miss.

President Kennedy announced Meredith's residence to the nation via a television press conference September 30, 1962.

The Klan and segregationists began entering the campus during day light hours September 30, 1962. U.S. Marshals were on campus. A riot which had been incited by Governor Ross Barnett turned into a full insurrection. JFK called in the National Guard and the army. The army had never been utilized to protect the rights of a citizen.

Two people were killed, and nearly 200 were injured during the Insurrection on the campus of the University of Mississippi, September 30, 1962.

October 1, 1962 James Meredith attended his first class.

He graduated August 18, 1963 obtaining a bachelor's degree in Political Science. The U.S. Marshals escorted Meredith and a caravan of supporters to Memphis.

One of the government's officials informed Meredith he was on the Klan's hit list and recommended he move out of the state.

Meredith relocated to Nigeria and enrolled in a masters degree program. He obtained a masters degree in Government and Economics from the University of Ibadan in 1965.

He and his family moved to Manhattan, and he enrolled in law school at Columbia University in 1965. His wife became a local school teacher.

On June 5, 1966, James Meredith started "Meredith Walk Against Fear," a 225 mile walk from the Tennessee-Mississippi line on Highway 51 to Jackson with 16 men. Some were from Memphis and a few travelled from NY.

Meredith sough to encourage blacks to register to vote, and to show black men they had nothing to fear by walking the highways and bi-ways in Mississippi.

On June 6, 1966, Meredith started off walking with a few NY friends in Hernando, Mississippi. Other men were planning to join them at another location in the county. The small group were followed by news reporter, a photographer, and several patrol cars.

Aubrey Norvell, a white male from Memphis spotted James Meredith walking, and ambushed him. Meredith was taken to a hospital in Memphis.

Dick Gregory flew his family to Memphis in his private plane to visit James Meredith. Gregory went to Hernando to the site of the shooting and decided to resume the walk.

Dr. Martin Luther King of SCLC, SNCC's Stokely Carmichael, and other leaders visited Meredith in the hospital and asked his permission to resume the walk which they renamed the Meredith March Against Fear. Gregory supported King and the other leaders.

Sunday, June 26, 1966 the march reached Tougaloo, Mississippi. James Brown performed on stage at Tougaloo College. People walked from Tougaloo College up State Street and other side streets to the State Capital in Jackson, Mississippi where speeches were presented from the back of a truck bed.

James Meredith received the loudest cheers. People cheered loudly with great excitement.

"The purpose of the march... to challenge that thing at the base of white supremacy - fear - fear that grips the Negro in America..." James H. Meredith said June 26, 1966.

His first memoir *Three Years in Mississippi* was published by Indiana University Press in 1966.

He later obtained the rights to *Three Years in Mississippi* from his publisher.

In 1979, Mary June died from heart failure.

In 1981, James Meredith married Judy Alsobrooks in Gary, Indiana.

He worked one-year tenures at a few jobs over his long career. He was a stock broker in NY, a visiting professor of African American Studies at the University of Cincinnati, taught at Thomas Christian Academy in Yazoo City, and served as a Domestic Advisor to Senator Jesse Helms.

While working in Washington, DC, Meredith conducted genealogy and historical research at the Library of Congress and used the data to self-published a volume of books.

To date he has published 27 works.

His latest memoir *A Mission from God: A Memoir and Challenge to America* was published by Simon and Schuster in 2012. His latest book, *The Ten Commandments* was self-published.

Over the years he launched walks to the library, walked to support HIV, immigrants, and in 2009 he launched the Meredith Walk for the Poor through the Mississippi Delta.

He is a self-made business man, an author of many books, an education pioneer, and now a devoted grandfather.

RESOLUTION OF RESPECT FOR GEORGE WASHINGTON GRAY

On behalf of the family of James Howard Meredith, we wish to express our gratitude and respect for Gray, who so valiantly stood guard to protect Meredith who was in the midst of a violent insurrection initiated by white southerners against the United States of American over Meredith's enrollment as the first Negro to an all-white college in the State of Mississippi, namely the University of Mississippi at Oxford, during the Jim Crow south for the fall semester in the year of our Lord nineteen hundred and sixty two.

We therefore acknowledge that according to his tender mercy, God, who is infinite in his wisdom, has seen fit to move from our presence a native son of the Great State of Mississippi, a soldier, and a remarkable citizen.

WHEREAS, our brother having been born on the ninth of June nineteen hundred and thirty-seven was raised by his loving parents in Charleston, Mississippi in the Delta.

WHEREAS, our brother registered to serve in the Army Reserve at the Charleston Court House during his senior year at Charleston Training School to comply with the Reserve Forces Act of 1955 which was signed into law by President Dwight David Eisenhower.

WHEREAS, brother Gray and his military company were called into action from Fort Benning, Georgia by a Proclamation and Executive Order issued by President John Fitzgerald Kennedy on September the thirtieth in the year of our Lord nineteen hundred and sixty two to force the Governor of the State of Mississippi and other persons who by unlawful assembly and whose actions were obstructing the enforcement of court orders to enroll James Meredith into college.

WHEREAS, Gray served twenty-six years in the Army and retired with honors in Fort Eustis, Virginia on September the thirtieth in the year of our Lord nineteen hundred and eighty three.

WHEREAS, brother Gray was a devoted husband and father who provided for his family and leaves here on earth a bright and exemplary example of good citizenship.

Therefore be it resolved that the Meredith family mourns with the family because we have a common bond of statehood and brotherhood with George Washington Gray.

Humbly submitted by Meredith Coleman McGee, a niece of James Howard Meredith, and the author of the biography *James Meredith: Warrior and the America that created him.*

____

Signed this fifth day of December two thousand and thirteen

Why Editors Select Flawed Free Manuscripts

By Meredith Coleman McGee, Publisher/Acquisition Editor, Meredith *Etc* www.meredithetc.com

August 27, 2015

As an acquisition editor, I attempt to acquire manuscripts for publication with potential sales power.

You may remember the bestselling novel *Gone With The Wind,* written by Margaret Mitchell, an Atlanta newspaper reporter. Her 1,036 page manuscript was not well organized. However, an editor thumped through the pages, fell in love with the story, and spent the next year guiding Mitchell's reorganization of her work.

Shortly after publication in 1936, the character Scarlett O'Hara captured the attention of 176,000 readers. Four years later, the book was converted into a film. Book sales climbed. John Grisham, James Patterson, Terry McMillan, and other writers have blossomed in the publishing industry too.

Today, editors seldom select manuscripts with severe structural problems because it takes a lot of time to revise flawed manuscripts.

In the era of print on demand, writers must produce well written manuscripts to get the attention of readers which equates into sales.

For starters, writers must avoid overusing words such as, "that," and "so." I requested an author remove "that" over 100 times, and delete 75 instances of "so" in a manuscript when I first got into this industry.

Fiction stories need strong characterization, and should avoid critical flaws. In general, writers are too close to their story to detect manuscript imperfections.

For example, a [normal] character cannot wear a full length fur coat in Palm Beach, Florida on Thanksgiving, or an arresting officer cannot hand cuff a fugitive outside of his jurisdiction. Stories must be believable and factual. Pres. Dwight D. Eisenhower was a five-star general in the U.S. Army during WWII. A "WWI" typo should be corrected.

A good editorial review will suggest authors have characters dress appropriate for 70 degree weather on Christmas in Miami, Florida.

Manuscripts must follow style rules. Chicago Manual of Style rules differ from APA or MLA. Chicago requires manuscripts cite the page number for statistical sources (250 million bales) in the form of notes. Marcus's coat is the proper possession citation of a word ending in "s" for Chicago, while "Marcus' coat" satisfies APA.

Writers must follow style rules, become fact checkers, and eliminate manuscript errors.

A good editorial review is much more than spelling and grammar. In the end, readers are attracted to polished stories.

Meredith Coleman McGee is an author, publisher, editor, and blogger. She is the author of *Nashida: Visits the Mississippi State Capitol, Nashida: Visits the Smith Robertson Museum*, *Odyssey*, *James Meredith: Warrior and the America that created him*, and the coauthor of *Married to Sin (Casada al Pecado - Spanish)*.

McGee is the acquisition editor of Meredith Etc, www.meredithetc.com, and the blog administrator of www.shopheirs.com. She was previously the acquisition editor at Mose Dantzler Press www.mosedpress.com.

https://meredithetc.com/meredith-coleman-mcgee/
This article was submitted to a writing blog.

November 14, 2016

NEWS

For immediate release – Jackson, Mississippi

Jacksonians seek to form the 1st Ever Friends of the Richard Wright Library

In light of the Jackson Hinds Library Systems' budget woos which presents book deserts in many key libraries in the city, Business Woman Meredith Coleman McGee, a niece of Civil Right icon James Meredith launched the **Campaign to form the Friends of the Richard Wright Library** last month.

As McGee noted in a one-on-one meeting Monday afternoon, October 24th with Patty Furr, Executive Director, Jackson Hinds Library Systems, "I'm not alone."

McGee was referring to Ercilla Hendrix, wife of Ward 6 Councilman Tyrone Hendrix, mother of two; Starkishia Rountree, Healthcare Professional, Author, mother of four; Loretha Wallace, mother of four, grandmother of 11; Businessman Timothy Stamps, Stamps Super Burgers; and Attorney Jovaunda Smith, daughter of Dr. Robert Smith, who desire to become founding members of this volunteer board.

A dubious policy is standing in their way. It dictates that the **Jackson Friends of the Library** which was created by the late Dr. Ollie Shirley and other concerned citizens in 1985, is the sole volunteer body charged with the task of raising funds for all eight (8) libraries in the city.

We, backed by the people, feel this policy must be changed. In fact, we support the formation of independent Friends' bodies for any of the eight (8) branches in the Great City of Jackson to rid this city of book desserts henceforth and forevermore. Strong library services can encourage reading and literacy.

For now, we are collecting petition signatures, obtaining letters and or statements of support, while administration is prolonging the *inevitable* – one Friends group for the entire city will not stand. Community needs vary from neighborhood to neighborhood, and volunteer boards can better capture the diverse needs of library patrons. School failure and library shortages are catastrophic. ###

The citizens were not allowed to form a second Friends Group. McGee, Loretha Wallace, Danielle Bogan, Hazel Janell Meredith (Hazel Hall), Starkishia Rountree, Vickie Jenkins, and Brenda Hyde launched the Community Library Initiative in 2017. So far, they developed the *My First Book Series* to promote early childhood learning and to raise funds. In 2017, the Department of Education attempted to take over the Jackson Public School system and two of the city's eight libraries closed. The group held a Spring Break Reading Fair at Pearl Street A.M.E Church in 2018. Lastly, the participants of the Reading Fair formed the *Learning Tree Book Club* and meet at the Jackson Medical Mall on the first Saturday of every month. The youngest book club member is six-years-old.

For more information or to make a donation the Community Library Initiative visit https://shopheirs.com/community-library-initiative/. Like the Facebook pages too https://www.facebook.com/community.library.ms/. To order the *My First Book Series* visit https://www.facebook.com/myfirstbookseries/.

References

Coleman, M. (March 17- 23, 1994). Historically black university in Jackson, Miss. to present television programming to local area, *Jackson Advocate*, 3A.

Coleman, M. (August 21- 27, 1997). Overcrowded schools top priority of new superintendent, *Jackson Advocate*, 5A.

McGee, Meredith. C. (Nov. 9-15, 2017). Authors face discrimination when attempting to get published in MS," *Jackson Advocate*, 6A.

McGee, Meredith. C. (June 15-21, 2004). Be patient when starting a new business, *Jackson Advocate*, 11A.

McGee, M. C. (July 1-7, 2004). Career advice, marketable resumes. *Jackson Advocate*, 11A.

McGee, M. C. (June, 2009). *Civil Rights icon's vision for the poor*. Published online. Meredithetc.biz

McGee, Meredith. C. (May 17-23, 2012). College grads end up with more than just a diploma in their hands, *Jackson Advocate*, 1A, 14A.

McGee, Meredith. C. (May 31 – June 6, 2012). Galloway students receive sound advice from Merritt, *Jackson Advocate*, 12A.

McGee, Meredith. C. (May. 31-June 6, 2012). Historic walk teaches basic principle, *Jackson Advocate*, 1A, 14A.

McGee, M. C. (June 24-30, 2004). How Can African Americans Compete in Today's Job Market? *Jackson Advocate*, 11A.

McGee, Meredith. C. (June 25-July 1, 2009). Last 2 miles of Meredith's Walk for the Poor, *Jackson Advocate*, 3A.

McGee, M. C. (July 1-7, 2004). Meredith on the road. *Jackson Advocate*, 11A.

McGee, Meredith. C. (August 9 - 15, 2012). Mississippi's Got Talent, *Jackson Advocate*, 2A.

McGee, Meredith. C. (Nov. 9-15, 2017). PTA at Mississippi's top school raising funds to Money, fees, and your future, *Jackson Advocate*, 3A, 10A.

McGee, Meredith. C. (May 31- June 6, 2012). Sykes honors 74 students headed to middle school, *Jackson Advocate*, 12A.

McGee, M. C. (29 May 2009). 200 miles for the poor and powerless. *The Mississippi Link*, http://themississippilink.com/.

SOMETHING STUDIED

This chapter contains a study which compared the characteristics and strategies of successful small business leaders in three southern states with prominent business leaders Sam Walton (Walmart), Ray Kroc (McDonalds), and Dave Thomas (Wendy's). The author completed this capstone project while pursuing a masters degree in Rural Community Development & Public Policy from Antioch University McGregor (renamed Antioch University Midwest) in Yellow Springs, Ohio.

Characteristics and Strategies of Successful Small Business Leaders

A Capstone Project
Presented to Antioch University McGregor
(Now known as Antioch University Midwest)

In Partial Fulfillment
For the Master of Arts Degree

By Meredith C. McGee

Jackson, Mississippi
Hinds County ▪ June 2004 ▪ Oct. 2013 ▪ March 2018

Ophelia Kelley, EdD, *Degree Committee Chair*
Brenda Hyde, MPPA, *Degree Committee Member*
Virginia Paget, PhD, *Faculty Advisor*

QUOTES & HIGHLIGHTS

- *Leaders are visionaries, who are both learners and teachers.*

- *Influence is the true measure of leadership.*

- *Effective leaders tend to be low in sentimental attachments and comfortable with criticism.*

- *Sam Walton believed that happy employees meant happy customers and more sales.*

- *The new currency of the Internet Age includes (social capital) which is the collective value of the people we know and what we can do for each other.*

- *More can be accomplished by empowering others than by ruling others.*

- *The relationship between leaders and subordinates is the number one success factor of a firm.*

- *Ray Kroc made a lot of sacrifices after becoming a partner with Dick and Maurice McDonald in 1955. Kroc worked long hours even though he was in his mid-fifties and he withheld his salary for eight years.*

- *Brain power is essential to succeed in the new economy. Making something happen is a function of what we know and who we know.*

Acknowledgements

This study was made easier because of the great support my husband and family extended to me. Dr. Ophelia Kelley, Degree Committee Chairman, and Brenda Hyde, Degree Committee gave me enormous support. I adore my academic advisor, Dr. Virginia Paget, who approved my Capstone Proposal to conduct research on small business leaders - a topic dear to my heart.

I earned this Individualized Masters degree in Rural Community Development & Public Policy as a participant in the Rural Development Leadership Network (RDLN). I would especially like to thank Shirley Sherrod and the Federation of Southern Cooperatives/Land Assistance Fund for supporting my first field project with the Family Farmers Cooperative. Also I extend my gratitude to Hollis Watkins, President, Southern Echo, Inc. for his assistance as my field advisor over my field project to facilitate redistricting trainings and to develop learning resources and new demography exercises.

My deepest regards are extended to Alice Thomas-Tisdale, Associate Publisher of the *Jackson Advocate* and Judy Alsobrooks, General Manager of W23BC Jackson State University for nurturing my early writing skills.

This study was possible because of the participation of 12 small business leaders who reside in Georgia, Mississippi, and Tennessee. I send my warm felt thanks to each business entrepreneur and manager who provided rich information to this study. Also I wish them continued success in their future business endeavors.

In addition, I am grateful to be the recipient of the first Billie Jean Young Scholarship award, named for the founding chairwoman of RDLN. Young is an organizer, poet, dramatist, and the creator of a one-woman show based on the life of Fannie Lou Hamer. I also appreciate the support I received from the U.S. Department of Agriculture.

RDLN has exposed me to a variety of rural communities in this country. Through this affiliation, I toured California's Central Valley, held discussions with California Hispanic farm workers, visited the Flathead Indian Reservation in Montana, attended writing, community development, marketing, and other workshops including a month-long institute at the University of California at Davis, and gained a broad perspective of rural America.

I am thankful to Starry Krueger, Founder/President RDLN, and to the many rural fellows who have obtained an individualized degree before me, and I will be grateful to those who are yet to follow this path. Thank you!

CAPSTONE ABSTRACT

Characteristics and Business Strategies of Successful Small Business Leaders

Meredith C. McGee

1. *Characteristics and Business Strategies of Successful Small Business Leaders* is a study that describes the leadership traits and business practices of successful small business owners and managers.

2. This study has great merit to me as an emerging service business owner and it is also relevant to other small business owners, managers, and leaders who may gain new insight from the findings.

3. This study discovered that some common characteristics and business strategies of effective small business leaders include displaying warmth to subordinates, possessing great interpersonal skills, being honest and fair, working hard, being persistent, being organized and setting goals, maintaining great client/customer relations, being open-minded and willing to learn new ideas, and maintaining control over financial matters. The data and the literature discovered these findings and more.

This study will address the following research question:

1. What are the characteristics and business strategies of successful small business leaders?

Effective small business owners and managers contribute to the success of their business and to our economy. According to the

2000 Census Statistics, 96.7% of Mississippi's businesses were small, and they employed 47.8% of the state's employees.

The research participants were required to have been in business for at least five years and to reside in the South. The business owners and leaders who participated in this study have been self-employed or in their leadership roles on average for 20 years, and their ages ranged from 40-70 years.

This study analyses the data collected from 12 small business entrepreneurs and managers. They have provided insight on what they consider the distinct characteristics and business strategies of successful small business leaders. The data corroborated with current literature.

TABLE OF CONTENTS

I. INTRODUCTION

This study is based on interviews with twelve small business entrepreneurs and managers who live in Georgia, Mississippi, and Tennessee. These leaders described their own behavior and how they manage and operate their small businesses. Their reflections on their leadership styles and business techniques have been compared to other successful leadership styles and business techniques suggested in the popular and scholarly literature.

A small business is defined as a firm with fewer than 500 employees in all of the industries or business locations in which the firm operates (Head, 2000, p. 13). Accordingly, Head said small businesses represented 99% of employers, employed half of the private sector workforce, and were responsible for around two-thirds to three-quarters of the net new jobs. In 2002, there were 22.9 million businesses in America and there were 18.4 million sole proprietorships.

Micro-businesses, which include the self-employed, the proverbial "mom and pop" shops, and most Main Street businesses, represent the majority, roughly 75 percent, of all businesses. Small businesses with five to 248 employees comprise about 25 percent of all businesses, while larger businesses represent one percent or less of all businesses (Zeuli & O'Shea, 16, 2017)

Williams (2004) said a 41-year-old national holiday "National Small Business Week" commences each May in honor of small businesses. Small Business Administration threw its annual party in honor of the holiday in Orlando, Florida, May 17 -21, 2004. Small businesses should be honored because they play large roles in our economy and they are great contributors of America's innovations.

Williams reported that small businesses made up 97% of the exporters during the 2001 fiscal year and that small businesses employ 39% of America's high-tech workers such as scientists and computer specialists.

According to Emmott (2004), the pacemaker, the personal computer, the Polaroid camera, and pre-stressed concrete all emerged from small businesses. In addition, Dell, Toyota, and

Walmart rose to the top of their particular industries by coming up with ways to get their products into the hands of consumers cheaper than their rivals.

The purpose of this study is to identify the leadership traits and business strategies of effective and successful small business owners and managers. This study uses the term leader to refer to the owner and or manager of a small business.

A criterion was established requiring research participants to have been in business or in their leadership role for at least five years. This report found that being honest, energetic, kind, goal oriented, fiscally responsible, open minded, willing to learn, and team oriented were common characteristics and practices of effective and successful business leaders.

One common characteristic that emerged from the data is the importance leaders place on respecting clients, customers, and employees. Kouzes & Posner (2003) stated that the relationship between leaders and subordinates (employees, volunteers) is the number one success factor of a business enterprise. Isidro (2001) agreed that entrepreneurs should treat customers well.

Characteristics and Business Strategies of Successful Small Business Leaders will address the following question:

1. What are the characteristics and business strategies of an effective and successful small business leader?

Business success can be described by a business' ability to reach several financial stages. However, Rodriguez (2003) contended that business success is hard to define and that success is not an overnight accomplishment. A business passes several milestones before proving it is on the right track. Rodriguez (2003) bases his findings from data collected from entrepreneurs concerning how they defined success. Several milestones indicate a business is on the way to success include the following markers:

1. Achieving the break-even point.
2. Earning a living wage, and

3. Achieving a real profit.

The breakeven point occurs when a business's expenses are equal to its revenues. At this stage, profit is zero. However, the paycheck for a business proprietor is profit. At the next level, a business owner is earning enough to yield a living or a respectable wage which can be similar to drawing a paycheck. However, there is nothing left over after the owner takes care of normal living expenses. When the business becomes successful, investments are generating real profits. At this stage, the business is more valuable than its assets; the enterprise is generating a return on investment and has a positive cash flow. Real profit equals business success.

Fulbright (2003) pointed out that every business success story starts with a big dream. According to Fulbright a study revealed that successful entrepreneurs share various characteristics such as working hard, being open to learning, being disciplined, having a vision, and being passionate about work tasks.

One's ability to set goals and plans for success are skills required to succeed. Fulbright (2003) maintained that failure is guaranteed if one does not plan. Studies show that many self-made millionaires have average intelligence, but they are willing to learn in order to achieve their financial goals.

Edmond Jr. (2004) abstracted four rules of business success from the popular TV series *The Apprentice*. The first lesson is that good ideas are not enough. A team must follow through with a plan. Edmond reasoned that business is like a game of chess, the person who thinks the furthest ahead has the most control over the future outcomes. He pointed out that Kwane Jackson's team was defeated in Donald Trump's business competition game because of poor planning.

According to Wendy's International, Inc.'s Website (2003), Dave Thomas, who founded Wendy's International, Inc., was a self-made millionaire. Hard work, dedication, and a commitment to learn the restaurant business helped him succeed.

Wendy's International Inc.'s Website said that Thomas did not have a high school diploma when he moved through the ranks of the restaurant business. Thomas started working in the industry at the age of 12 and he dropped out of school when he was 15 to work full-time at the Hobby House, where he met Colonel Sanders, founder of Kentucky Fried Chicken. In 1962, Thomas was given the opportunity to turn four failing Kentucky Fried Chicken restaurants (now KFC) around. Equipped with knowledge of the restaurant business, he was successful. He was given a million-dollar commission for turning the restaurants around, becoming a millionaire at age 35.

According to the U.S. Small Business Administration (2002) today's leaders are visionaries. They are both learners and teachers, who foresee paradigm changes in society. The increasing rate of change in the business environment is a key reason for a new emphasis on leadership. A renewed focus on leadership emerged after the turn of this century. No longer are managers expected to maintain the status quo to move business forward. Today's marketplace has changed this narrow focus.

Taylor (2004) reported that the American Management Association which was formed in 1923 taught the principle of "scientific management" and shaped our early understanding of the role of industrial leaders. During the second half of the last century, the Center for Creative Leadership opened and a wave of university-based education programs were created. Taylor said there are currently over 59,000 book titles under the heading of "Leadership." By 2018, the print-on-demand era, there were over 100,000 books listed on leadership in Amazon's online database.

Kouzes & Posner (2003) said that the term 'lead' is an old English word meaning go, travel, and guide. From this definition, I imagine that a leader's role resembles that of a tour guide. Kouzes & Posner (2002) defined leadership as the long-term development of people and organizations so that they can adapt, change, thrive, and grow.

Maxwell (2002) claimed leadership has many facets which include "respect, experience, emotional strength, interpersonal skills, discipline, vision, perseverance, and influence (p. 13)." The interviewees described many of these characteristics.

The U.S. Small Business Administration pointed out that effective leaders tend to be low in sentimental attachments and comfortable with criticism. In addition, they are in general poised and relatively insensitive to hardships. The research participants also mentioned that leaders should accept constructive criticism. The U.S. Small Business Administration suggested that it is important for leaders to accept criticism, while McCauley, Moxley, and Velsor (1998) contended that a supervisor who offers a subordinate constructive criticism also contributes to his or her development and growth.

The data derived from the interviewees also stress the need to engage in on-the-job training and the need for training in general. The data suggest that job training and other formal trainings help individuals grow professionally.

McCauley et al. stated that the first year of a new job is generally more developmental for an individual than the fifth year of employment. Likewise, a practical training program that helps participants examine mistakes is more developmental than one that gives information but no practice. Assessment, challenge, and support are ingredients that enrich one's professional development.

Hoffman (2004) described one California firm's leadership training program as an ongoing self-improvement process that empowers career growth. This California-based company uses an intranet skills assessment exam to determine the learning needs of information technology managers. Once their learning needs have been assessed, managers are required to participate in classroom trainings, online courses, read selected books, or engage in other activities.

Characteristics and Business Strategies of Successful Small Business Leaders will describe the common attributes and business strategies of effective and successful small business leaders. These characteristics and other findings will be discussed further in this study.

II. LITERATURE REVIEW

This section of the capstone project will discuss some fundamental characteristics and business strategies of effective and successful small business leaders. Maxwell (2002) said influence is the true measure of leadership. Kouzes & Posner (2002) described five leadership practices which include modeling the way, inspiring a shared vision, challenging the process, enabling others to act, and encouraging the heart.

Kouzes & Posner asserted that a leader's behavior wins him or her respect and inspires others to see new opportunities in the future. Leaders are also pioneers and creators of innovation who foster collaboration and trust, and shared leadership. Kouzes & Posner claim their studies have shown that effective leaders use these five principles to lead their organizations to new heights.

Maxwell (2002) developed a leadership principle called: The Law of the Lid. He asserted this concept helps people understand the value of leadership. Maxwell alleged that leadership ability is the lid that determines a person's level of effectiveness. He claimed that the lower a person's ability to lead, the lower the lid on his potential. However, the more influence one's leadership has, the greater the effectiveness of that individual.

Maxwell told the story of the famous McDonald brothers to illustrate the Law of the Lid. In 1930, Dick and Maurice McDonald moved to California to pursue employment opportunities. When Dick and Maurice arrived in Hollywood they started working at a movie studio and eventually they opened a theater in Glendale. By 1937, the brothers opened a small drive-in restaurant in Pasadena. Their customers parked outside the restaurant in their cars; they would receive their food and beverages (hotdogs, fries, and milkshake) on trays complete with china plates, glassware and metal utensils.

In 1940, Dick and Maurice moved their successful restaurant business to Bernardino. The menu was expanded to include sandwiches, hamburgers, and other items. Eight years later, they were serving only walk-in customers, had eliminated the china, glassware, and metal utensils with paper products, and had turned their kitchen into an assembly line. By the mid-1950's, their net profits were around $100,000 each. The neon sign outside the restaurant said McDonald's Hamburgers.

In 1954, the McDonald brothers partnered with Ray Kroc who sold and serviced their milk shake machine. Kroc had a vision of the restaurant serving hundreds of markets nationally. He entered into a partnership with the brothers in 1955. The business was renamed McDonald's System, Inc. and later called the McDonald's Corporation.

In pursuit of his dreams, Kroc worked without a salary for several years and borrowed money from his life insurance policy to pay key employees. His sacrifices paid off and in 1961, Kroc purchased the exclusive rights to McDonald's and turned it into a global entity. Maxwell (2002) pointed out that the "lid" in the life and leadership of Kroc was much greater than the lid of Dick and Maurice McDonald. The brothers were only instrumental in obtaining 15 franchise contracts, whereas Kroc obtained 100 contracts over a four-year period.

By 1963, there were 500 McDonald's. According to the McDonald's Corporation's Website (2004), today there are more than 30,000 McDonald franchises in over 119 countries serving 47 million customers daily.

Maxwell (2002) alleges that personal success without leadership ability limits one's effectiveness. Maxwell claimed that a person's impact depends on his leadership ability. Accordingly, he maintained that McDonald's Corporation exists because of Kroc's leadership effectiveness.

Dick and Maurice McDonald created the restaurant model for McDonald's Hamburgers. However, Kroc's leadership and influence paved the path that allowed the corporation to reach hundreds of markets which led to the corporation becoming an international franchise.

Sam Walton was an effective leader too. According to the Little Rock, Arkansas Website (2004), Walmart's founder Sam Walton lived by a set of business principles he called the Ten Commandments of Retail. The commandments are as follows:

1. Commit to your goals.
2. Share your rewards.
3. Energize your colleagues.
4. Communicate all you know.
5. Value your associates.
6. Celebrate your success.
7. Listen to everyone.
8. Deliver more than you promise.
9. Work smarter than others, and
10. Blaze your own path (p. 1-2).

Walton was born in Kingfish, Oklahoma in 1918. His first retail experience was working at his father's store in Missouri where he was reared and attended school. After graduating from college in 1940, Walton opened a Ben Franklin Five and Dime franchise in Arkansas. In 1962, Walton opened his first Walmart store in Rogers, Arkansas. The store specialized in low prices and was successful.

Little Rock, Arkansas Website added that Walton's managerial style was popular with employees and some of the basic concepts he founded exists today such as profit sharing. Walton believed that happy employees meant happy customers and more sales. He was also an advocate of team work. Today, Walmart gives employee discounts and stock options. By 1991, there were 1,700 Walmart stores. At the time of Walton's death in 1992, he was the world's second richest man. William "Bill" Gates was the richest man (Little Rock, Arkansas Website, 2004, p. 1).

Isidro (2001) maintained that the latest data showed service businesses achieved nearly $3 trillion in revenue in 1998. The success or failure of a service business depends on the firm's leadership ability to reach and maintain the right customers. To begin with, the key to good client relations is to discover client expectations. Maintaining a record of client needs and wants is very helpful.

Isidro (2001) advised entrepreneurs not to regret ending a relationship with an over-demanding client, because such clients can create stressful working relationships which have negative impacts on leaders. However, she suggested that leaders keep accounts that will contribute to business growth.

Wendy's International, Inc. (2003) said Dave Thomas founded Wendy's International, Inc. at the age of 37 in 1969, which was less than three years after he became a millionaire. The restaurant was named after his daughter. One of his priorities was customer service. Like the McDonald brothers, Thomas created an innovative quick service restaurant approach. The restaurants served fresh ground beef, square patties, which were made-to-order. Thomas also introduced the salad bar and baked potatoes on a national level. Thomas said, "If we take care of our customers every day and exceed their expectations, we'll earn their loyalty" (p. 2). Thomas lived by five values which include:

1. Quality is our Recipe.
2. Do the Right Thing.
3. Treat People with Respect.
4. Profit is Not a Dirty Word, and
5. Giving Back.

As did other effective leaders, Thomas lived by the golden rule. He also stressed the importance of being honest, having integrity, and giving back. His favorite charity was supporting adoption causes since Thomas himself had been adopted when he was six-weeks-old. Williams (2004) reported that small businesses contribute millions of dollars yearly to their communities. Williams noted that the Princeton Survey Research Associates said "91% of businesses with four to 99 employees support local charities and groups" (p. 39).

Kouzes & Posner (2002) said connecting others to sources of power is important. The new currency of the Internet Age includes *social capital* which is the collective value of the people we know and what we can do for each other. Leaders must make networking a part of their agenda by linking to the sources of information, resources, and influence needed to make things happen. Fulbright (2003) agreed that small businesses always need assistance which can be obtained through networking.

The U.S. Small Business Administration (2003) used a personality assessment of military leaders designed by Raymond Cattell in 1954 to characterize effective leaders. Cattell developed a list of traits that effective leaders possess based on a study he conducted on military leaders. The list of traits for effective leaders includes the following:

1. Emotional stability. Leaders must be able to handle stress.
2. Dominance. Leaders are able to overcome obstacles.
3. Enthusiasm. Leaders are optimistic.
4. Conscientiousness. Leaders usually have a high standard of excellence.
5. Social boldness. Leaders are socially aggressive and tend to be high in emotional stamina.
6. Tough-mindedness. Leaders are practical, logical, and to-the-point.
7. Self-assurance. Leaders are self-confident.
8. Compulsiveness. Leaders have great foresight and are very careful decision makers.

In addition, leaders of today must motivate others and lead them in new directions. They must also be able to envision the future. Effective leaders must place personal power secondary to the development of subordinates. More can be accomplished by empowering others than by ruling others. Empathy is also an important trait of leaders. They must be able to put themselves in the shoes of others. Team orientation is also important. Leaders must have charisma. They must be able to arouse the emotions of others. Effective leaders usually have *larger than life* personalities.

Planning control mechanisms is as important to business success as setting goals and planning. Wijewardena, Zoysa, Fonseka, and Perera (2004) claimed there is a relationship between planning sophistication and the performance of small enterprises. Enterprises should use "control processes" which is a method of measuring actual performance against planned performance from time to time to analyze any deviations from a plan. Strategic planning is the most sophisticated form of business planning which is also connected to a company's performance.

In addition to planning, U.S. Small Business Administration (2002) considered empathy to be a characteristic of an effective leader. Being able to "put yourself in the other person's shoes" is an important trait (p. 2). Humility like empathy is a vital trait of an effective leader. Doty (2000) defined humility as the quality of genuine modesty and unpretentiousness (p. 89). Doty pointed out that the humble leader lacks arrogance which has nothing to do with lacking aggressiveness. Since the U.S. military has to deal with diverse cultures to negotiate peace agreements, Doty assumed that it is important for leaders to be able to maintain a certain level of humility, because loud, obnoxious, arrogant communications will not achieve a compromise during a town meeting between Albanians and Serbs.

Doty (2000) added that success is all in relation to a "team" and "we," not "you" and "me." Hence, an effective leader understands that success is for the unit as opposed to success being connected to individual achievement.

Lauer (2002) claimed that many companies who have filed Chapter 11 (bankruptcy), have arrogant leaders behind the failure of the business. Lauer said arrogant leaders forget to acknowledge their colleagues who do the heavy lifting and make them look good. He proclaimed that every quality leader should have the indefinable trait of "humility."

Hoffman (2004) claimed strong managers have good coaching, communication, and conflict resolution skills; they also have knowledge of human resource policies. Hoffman also said that some success factors include a manager's understanding of leadership functions such as team-building, budgeting, and how to comply with employment laws.

Women Today Magazine (2004) listed seven traits of effective leaders. These characteristics have been drawn from information provided by other experts. The seven specific actions that experts say successful leaders carry out include the following:

1. Emphasize the strengths and contributions of others.

2. Promote a vision that will become valuable to others.
3. Treat followers the way you enjoy being treated.
4. Admit mistakes because leaders who hide mistakes encourage subordinates to hide their mistakes.
5. Criticize others only in private because public criticism alienates people.
6. Talk to people, ask questions, and visit worksites.
7. Set team goals and reward people who meet and exceed them.

Kouzes & Posner (2002) said when a leader admits his or her mistake he or she builds credibility rather than damages credibility. They added that admitting mistakes connects to the concept, "Don't expect perfection; do expect dedication" (p. 233). The first time someone makes a mistake, we say, "He's still learning." The second time, we say, "Slow learner." The third time it's "He'll never learn!" In terms of mistakes, people usually apply the American metaphor, "three strikes and you're out!" (p. 234).

Honesty and encouraging others are essential leadership strategies too. Kouzes & Posner (2003) declared that encouragement is an ingredient that will sustain an employee's commitment to an organization. Kouzes & Posner said "The word "recognize" is a Latin term which means to know again, (p. 19)." Recognitions are reminders and ways to show subordinates what an organization values.

Kouzes & Posner (2003) proclaimed that during their years of research, they discovered that the relationship between leaders and subordinates is the number one success factor of a firm. One survey instrument showed that the highest performing companies had managers who were warm and who showed fondness toward others. Encouraging others also improves performance.

Another study showed that 98% of employees said they performed at higher levels when they are encouraged by their supervisors. Kouzes & Posner also noted that another survey conducted by the Kepner-Tregroe study showed that 96% of participants stated "I get a lot of satisfaction out of knowing I've done a good job" (p. 4). Being warm and objective are significant characteristics of effective leaders.

The authors said another study conducted with youth participants showed that subordinates felt a superior's ability to see a situation from someone else's point of view was the most important quality a leader could possess.

Taylor (2004) pointed out that a comprehensive study conducted by Talent Keepers of 40,000 workers showed that employees wanted leaders whom they could trust, treated them fairly, and showed care and concern for them. Cynthia McCauley, a senior fellow at the Center for Creative Leadership, commented in the article that building trusting and positive relationships is a key element in gaining staff commitment.

Recognizing subordinates is a company's opportunity to say to them, "I'd like to remind you one more time what is important around here" (Kouzes & Posner, p. 19). To illustrate this point, Kouzes & Posner described an incident where a factory worker was rewarded and the company manager reiterated that the worker had followed the company's "no reject" policy. The worker had discovered a way to melt a defective product as opposed to rejecting the product and discarding it.

According to Kouzes & Posner (2003), even a simple "Thank you" which is a non-financial award, is a great way to show appreciation at any given time. The following section will describe several methods of rewarding and recognizing subordinates or employees contributions to an organization or business.

Kouzes & Posner (2003) stated that The Oak Ridge National Laboratory connected performance with awards. This company uses a pin progression system to award employees. The colors of the pins were white, orange, green, blue, and red; red represented the highest honor. Leaders can describe their organizational values through award systems. Values set the stage for action and goals and allow staff to release energy.

Kouzes & Posner (2003) further added that it is important to know something about a person and his or her culture before recognizing his or her contributions or presenting him or her with a reward. Another story mentioned an administrative assistant who was presented with a silver jewelry tray as a reward for her 17 years of service. She loved the thought that went behind the gift, but personally disliked the color silver and was disappointed. The authors pointed out that leaders should investigate the likes and dislikes of awardees by talking to family, friends, and associates before preparing a special recognition event for someone.

Kouzes & Posner (2003) provided seven essential steps to encouraging others and they are listed below:

1. Set clear standards by making sure constituents understand the values and operating principles that are important for the organization.
2. Expect the best from subordinates by being positive and believing in their ability to make great contributions.
3. Pay attention to the work environments, employees and subordinates. Help someone complete one of his or her job assignments to gain an understanding of his or her job. Try to determine the needs and aspirations of constituents including how they like to be recognized and what makes them feel appreciated. Recognizing the anniversary and birthday of subordinates are also great ways to show appreciation.
4. Personalizing the recognition of others is important. Sending champagne or sparkling cider and flowers to the family of someone who deserves being rewarded is a way to personalize recognition.
5. The fifth essential step to encouraging others is telling a story about their contribution. A good story can create a sense of place.
6. Celebrating together is the next step. A celebration is a way to offer social support. It is also a means of honoring an individual or group for upholding specific organizational standards.
7. The seventh and last essential stage of encouragement is for leaders to set the example.

Buchanan (2001) asserted that employees are happy when management figures out what makes each employee tick. Buchanan (2001) agreed with Kouzes & Posner (2003) that subordinates are more receptive to personalized awards than they are to standard awards. Buchanan (2001) maintained that the 90 employees at Technology Professionals Corp. were assessed individually and then management recorded the information and gave out occasional customized rewards. Pre-paid funerals and ice cream treats were examples of the kinds of personalized awards this company gave to its employees.

During thirty day evaluations, employees were questioned about their hobbies, children, spouses, pets, among other things. This concept is called "Management one-to-one." Examples of creative award and recognition methods are below:

1. Hours as flexible as a Romanian gymnast,
2. Funding for staff engineers and scientists to deliver their non-work related research at far-flung professional conferences,
3. The services of an ergonomics consultant,
4. Textbook money for interns, and
5. The opportunity for employees to audition new chairs and desks in order to select the most comfortable.

Like Kouzes & Posner (2003), Buchanan (2001) pointed out that customizing recognition and award systems eliminated the waste and inefficiency of giving employees benefits they did not want nor need. The author also described another method of individualizing awards. He stated that each December, the CEO/Founder of a large corporation hand delivered over 3,000 cards. In the process of thanking staff for their contributions to the company, he asked each employee's opinion of how to improve the company.

The night before visiting a unit, the Founder read management reports to learn personalized information about each person. The Founder maintained that it takes him nearly one month to deliver all of the cards, but that he values what he learned about employee's attitudes, ideas, and suggestions during casual conversations.

Steven Lassig, a manager, said in the past he took employees and their spouses or significant others to dinner. Since his staff is much larger now, Lassig takes groups of people to lunch or dinner to intermingle. The socializing allows him to get to know each staff person and gives him ideas on how to individualize rewards.

Lassig (2001) stated that he engaged his staff in a contest to allow them to describe their ideal work environment. First prize was $5,000 and second prizes were several personal computers. He incorporated some of the suggestions into the company's personnel policies. The suggestions included giving employees the options of obtaining monetary performance awards, free housecleaning services, or airline tickets.

In addition to encouraging subordinates, leaders should display common courtesies. Isidro (2001) emphasized the need for entrepreneurs to follow the "golden rule" and also the importance of apologizing to clients when one is late delivering a service. These tips were abstracted to provide a guide to business owners on how to get clients to love and value their service. Jamison (1984) described behavior that leaders should not utilize. It is his assumption that negative remarks which he calls "nibbles" stunt professional growth.

Some examples of nibbles are as follows.

1. You ask too many questions.
2. You always give your ideas first.
3. Why don't you just stick to what you have to do, and we'll handle this.
4. You're too sensitive.
5. If I share my idea, I may embarrass myself.
6. What do you really know about it?
7. We've always done it this way.

Jamison (1984) assumed that nibbles are ways for leaders to remain bigger than others or ways for people who are afraid to grow to remain smaller than others. People are characterized as circles and examples of big circles include leaders, movers, shakers, and independent thinkers. Small circles are people who are second in command, responders, reactors, and even shy non-contributors. Jamison (1984) contended that once people understand that there is room for everyone to grow and get bigger, people will stop nibbling. He adds that power, like energy and light and love can expand infinitely.

Anderson (2003) developed a step-by-step guide to promoting professional growth. According to this guide, leaders should listen to their colleagues and pay attention to questions which are frequently asked. He also said leaders should assess their skills in order to develop the kinds of training programs to teach others. Anderson says short courses may have a higher success rate than longer formal training sessions. "Ten Minutes of Tech" on Tuesdays, Question and Answer sessions during lunch, or short evening classes are examples of quick sessions.

Staff development and growth are important to any organization; the need to assess and evaluate programs and progress are also critical. An assessment tool can be used to determine whether an employee benefited from a seminar or to determine how well a manager or an employee is performing.

Professional growth is one component of leadership development. According to Anderson (2003), leaders can help staff grow professional by spending quality time with employees, listening to their needs, and providing the opportunities for staff to learn by providing direct learning instructions and activities. Taylor (2004) pointed out that developing staff growth enhances an employee's commitment and loyalty.

Assessment tools can increase self-awareness by providing information to an individual concerning his or her strengths and weaknesses. The assessment component can answer the question, "How am I doing?" (McCauley et al., 1998, p. 37).

Vella, Berardinelli, and Burrow (1998) offered an approach to evaluating adult learning that is harmonious with the popular education approach. They said the purpose of evaluation (assessment) include the following.

1. To aid in the design of the program.

2. To provide feedback to learners/instructions during the program, and
3. To determine if learners developed important knowledge, skills, and attitudes as a result of the program.

Vella et al. (1998) also noted that evaluations should help determine whether learners were able to use what they learned after completing the program and to determine if the program had the impact on people and organizations that was anticipated.

Vella et al. stated several methods of evaluating learner performance included evaluating a learner's knowledge, skills, and attitudes. Oral questioning, discussions, writing assignments, class activities and assignments are ways to evaluate knowledge.

Vella et al. do not consider testing to be an effective means of gathering evaluation information because testing only measures learner performance. However, true-false, matching, listing, completion, multiple choice, short answer, essay, case studies, and problem solving are appropriate methods to evaluate one's knowledge base.

In addition, simulations of individual skills, completing tasks, games, projects, performance evaluations, and role playing are other ways to evaluate skills. Self-perceptions and the perception of customers, co-workers, supervisors, and peers and direct or discreet observations can be conducted to evaluate a person's attitude (Vella et al.).

Kouzes & Posner (2003) said not only should leaders use assessment tools to evaluate adult learning, but leaders should also get feedback on how well they encourage subordinates. These scholars proclaimed that the number one organizational success factor is the relationship between leaders and subordinates.

Leaders should also assess the attitudes of subordinates concerning organizational values. Kouzes & Posner (2002) said it is important for leaders to receive feedback and be evaluated by peers and subordinates concerning their leadership roles.

Smith (2000) favored giving employee's permission to disagree with management. Smith cautioned managers not to be afraid to have staff evaluate their performance. Smith reasoned that managers should ask often “What should I stop doing, what should I keep doing, and what I need to start doing? The use of assessment tools was recommended in the literature and was also suggested by the interviewees.

III. METHODOLOGY

The interview data were collected from the perspectives of 12 small business leaders, who have been in their leadership roles for an average of 20 years. Of the 12, two of them have been in business for five years, four have been in business for at least 10 years, and three of them have been in business at least 20 years. One of them has been a business proprietor for 27 years and another business owner has operated various ventures for nearly 50 years.

During the fall of 2003 and the winter of 2004, consent letters were mailed to 20 business leaders, who had been in their roles for at least five years and who resided in the South (Georgia, Mississippi, Tennessee). Of the 20 letters, 12 leaders were chosen for interviews. The consent forms gave them the option of being interviewed in-person or by some other method. The interview time ranged from 30 minutes to two hours.

Seven of the respondents were female and five of them were male. The interviewees were between 40 - 70 years of age. Eleven of the research participants owned and operated small businesses and one was a program director of a television station. Of the 12 interviewees, only two desired to be interviewed over the phone. One participant sent her interview response through an e-mail attachment and all of the other participants were interviewed in-person. No one gave consent to have their business space photographed.

Most of the business owners were sole proprietors. The leaders operated a range of small businesses including one real estate investment firm, three insurance agencies, one pest control business, one plumbing company, one hair styling salon, one real estate firm, one cleaning service, one car rental company, one sales business, and one weekly newspaper outlet.

Interview Responses

The following responses were obtained during the course of the interviews. Two of the interview questions that participants were asked are listed below.

1. Why did you start your business or accept your leadership role?
2. Describe your most memorable business mistakes.

A total of nine questions were asked and the full list is provided on page 235.

The owner of a cleaning service was the first interviewee. She replied that after obtaining a degree in Criminal Justice in 1979, a freeze on jobs occurred in her field. Having a daughter in college she and her husband were supporting financially, she needed an immediate income. Using one of her strongest assets and skills, she started a cleaning service.

The business proprietor recalled that the most important lessons she learned as a small business leader were that a business owner had to work hard, always watch out for pit falls, work long hours, and be aware that being in business is a learning process.

Opening her business with a degree did not negate the need to learn managerial skills. Therefore, after her business was established she acquired accounting, bookkeeping, payroll, tax preparation skills, and also learned how to manage a cleaning crew.

This participant recalled that it is important for employees to be able to take their child to the doctor and to take care of other personal needs and that flexible work hours enhanced and encouraged her staff to grow. This entrepreneur considered being honest, being on-time, having knowledge of one's business industry, having good relationships with the people one employs, and keeping promises as five effective leadership strategies.

One of her greatest business mistakes was hiring an accountant who almost placed her business in tax trouble. Treating staff and clients with respect and being courteous and honest are some of her priorities.

The second participant was a real estate investor who had been in business for over 20 years. She started investing in real estate because she was presented with the opportunity to purchase her first piece of property cheap. One of the greatest lessons this leader learned was the need to create a financial repair and maintenance reserve. When she started her business venture she had a master's degree in Early Childhood Education. Knowing how to keep books, plan strategically, and conduct task analysis served as a foundation when she was establishing her business. Over time, she learned how to do house repairs like painting, window replacement, and other maintenance.

When asked to state five leadership strategies, she replied, "public relations, respect, communication, listening, and people skills." The entrepreneur stated that difficult situations such as a conversation concerning an eviction should be approaching tactfully. This proprietor learned how to listen to the tenants' side of the story when problems arose because people appreciate being treated respectfully.

Failing to engage in long-range planning and not creating a cash reserve were some of her biggest mistakes. However, treating renters well were some of her greatest strengths which is why many of them maintain long-term leases. Living spaces are sanitized before a new leasee moves in. Carpet is replaced when it is worn out. Padlocks are used for security and special coloring is placed on the wall. This participant's interview ended after she described the special amenities that she used in the apartments.

Another research participant learned his trade before opening his business. After learning the pest control industry, a former pest control employee decided to start his own business to earn money, be able to control his future, and to be in a position to help people.

During his nine years in business, this business owner's most important lessons were how to deal with people and how to be open minded. Being able to solicit pest control business, supervise employees, and perform bookkeeping tasks were skills he possessed when he opened his business. As time passed, he learned how to prepare financial statements and how to market his services.

He also stated that money and raises enhanced and encouraged employees to grow.

He contended being on time, having good communication skills, putting forth a good personal appearance, and having a pleasant attitude are effective leadership strategies. Hiring family and friends were the greatest business mistakes he made. This business owner's managerial style was to share power. His approach was to make suggestions as opposed to demanding that tasks be carried out in a certain manner. For example, he would say, "I would do this task this way." This leader said he treats staff and customers very well.

A business partner who has operated a weekly newspaper for 24 years assumed her leadership role because she liked the idea of working in a flexible environment and being in a position to engage in community service work. Giving back to the community was one of the most important lessons she learned.

According to this newspaper entrepreneur, the role of a small business is important because they make up over 90% of all businesses and they are the pulse of America. She was equipped with a quality education, a business degree, and basic managerial skills when she assumed her leadership position at the newspaper enterprise. Her skills included balancing accounts, keeping books, and managing employees. Through experience she learned the importance of networking. In addition, on-the-job training enhanced her ability to operate the paper and also fine-tuned her managerial and other skills.

This business owner said a hands-off leadership structure enhances and encourages staff to grow. One of her assumptions is that staff should be encouraged to look at themselves and to realize their skills and talents. Newspaper staff are given the opportunity to engage in entrepreneurial side ventures, for example, résumé writing and graphic design projects. Management allows staff to earn extra money in an effort to allow them to grow professional and develop their business skills.

The newspaper manager's idea of effective leadership strategies included defining leadership and being an example for others to follow. She discovered that networking with others who had the same agenda is important. Effective communication systems create an atmosphere where people know what is going on as well as strengthens relationships.

Slow tax preparation, poor budgeting and ineffective promotional and marketing are some of the biggest mistakes the newspaper made during its early years of operation. For example, informing the public of the newspaper's community activities would have been in the newspaper's advantage, but instead leadership was silent.

The newspaper partner described her managerial style to be relaxed. The company is team oriented and one would not know she was in charge until pay day because she is a co-worker first. Customer service and family needs are very important to management. When an employee's child is sick, he or she is allowed to take his or her child to the doctor or to bring his or her child to work.

In addition, incentives and employer/employee relationships are important. Last year the staff and their family took a trip to Disney World. The office environment includes a lot of love. Like a family, staff members support each other when tragedies occur such as family illnesses.

The owner of a real estate firm became intrigued with the idea of being self-employed while in high school. Obtaining a degree in business administration, he worked several jobs, and eventually opened a real estate firm, which he has operated for the past 27 years. During that time, the lessons he learned included treating others as one would like to be treated. He concluded that honesty goes a lot further than dishonesty.

Having worked at General Motors Corporation, Sears, Roebuck & Co., and several other places provided this real estate business owner with managerial skills and sales experience. Over the years he acquired a number of business skills which were important because the scope of his business changed as the industry changed. This leader contended that financial, job training, and personal rewards enhance and encourage employees to grow.

This real estate proprietor regrets that he did not take full advantage of stock investments, bank instruments, and other financial tools; he considered this missed opportunity as his biggest business mistake. It is his assumption that a business will fail if a hands-on concept is not utilized and that a no-nonsense attitude is as necessary as treating staff and clients with respect.

A research participant who had been a small business leader for over 60 years was in the car rental business. He started his first business venture at the age of ten selling crickets and grasshoppers to fishermen. His father was a farmer and he liked farming. While in the military, he earned extra money by organizing car washes and running night clubs. This participant became self-employed because he liked being independent; he also admires capitalism which he contended is the most effective and fairest system in the world.

Listening skills and knowledge of fishing were this participant's strengths when he started his bait sales venture. He said fishermen paid dearly for the kind of crickets and grasshoppers they preferred. The knowledge of how to use money wisely and efficiently is some of the skills this leader acquired after being in business for a number of years.

The car rental entrepreneur's theory was that business failure is caused by poor judgment and managing money is very important. For example, one of his business ventures was a magazine business and because he understood the market, he would print 1000 copies of the magazine and sell nearly 1000 copies. He said the above example was an illustration of efficient use of resources and displayed good judgment.

He noted that businesses can't have employees they can't afford because they will steal or stop working. Being fair, being firm, paying employees enough money to take care of themselves are leadership strategies.

The car rental businessman assumed it is not wise for a business leader to make employees too smart and would like to chalk up his business mistakes to equal experience. He recalled that allowing subordinates to make decisions that they did not have the capacity to make were big mistakes. As a manager, he is an autocrat, who is single-handed and operates one way - his way. This leader stated, if subordinates have a better way they should start their own business.

According to this leader's theory, staff should do things the way the business leader desired things to operate and that subordinates should not manage business resources if he or she cannot manage his or her own resources. His treatment of customers depends on their status. The car rental businessman contended that very few creditors will do the right thing and collection accounts are handled differently from other accounts. People who have good standing accounts are treated accordingly.

Another interviewee was a general insurance agent who has operated a business for 10 years. Her father was a contractor and he influenced her to become self-employed. Having a belief in God and one's self are the most important business lessons she learned.

In addition, a business leader should be respectful, honest, fair, and willing to accept constructive criticism. When her insurance agency opened, her assets included knowledge and expertise in the insurance field, paralegal training, and clerical experience. Through the years, she acquired computer, Internet, and bookkeeping skills. This agent's professionalism and customer service skills also improved.

Being honest, displaying a cool demeanor, showing respect and appreciation for clients, returning phone calls, and being impartial and fair to all clients are her view of good leadership strategies. Staff growth is obtained in her view by income, hardwork, and persistence. On a scale of 1 to 10, she gives herself a 9, in terms of customer service and relations.

Another interviewee was the program director of a television station; she started an Internet business after realizing she could manage and develop programs for her own business start-up just as she had done for the television station. Reflecting over the years, she recalled that paying attention to details and selecting the right personnel and partners were the most important leadership lessons she learned.

This participant said she was equipped with a background in television programming including anchoring, assignment editing, management, interpersonal, and communication skills when she became the director of the station. This manager's strengths included the ability to set goals and be objective-oriented. In addition, she did not fear making decisions that where contrary to practices in the industry.

Work experiences improved her judgment to choose internal and external political battles and enhanced her negotiating and problem solving skills. Overtime she acquired the intuition to analyze teammates and act according to the political environment which decreased internal tensions.

This leader assumed that regular evaluations are important because people need to understand how they are doing professionally. An open door policy is implemented by this company which gives staff the opportunity to offer suggestions and to critique management. To enhance staff growth and development, staff is allowed to be creative, management respects the skills and talents that staff brought to the job to begin with, staff attends trainings and workshops, and micro-managerial tactics are avoided.

Maintaining an atmosphere in which staff can make decisions without fear of error, respecting staff as human beings first, and rewarding and recognizing their contributions are effective leadership strategies. One of this manager's greatest mistakes was not getting a second opinion on the cost of a repair. Obtaining another opinion would have prevented the station from losing air production time.

This manager shares leadership and decision making and utilizes a hands-off managerial approach. Staff, partners, and associates are treated with admiration and respect. Whether or not she is doing the right thing is always a consideration. Maintaining respectful communication during projects required tact and consideration. Untactful behavior like "going over someone's head can destroy trust and diminish progress," she said.

The owner of a plumbing company, who has done residential and commercial service for six years, started his business in an effort to build wealth. The most important lesson this participant learned was the need to have funds reserved for business expenses such as tools, supplies, and equipment rental. In addition, he learned to be fair to himself and charge the appropriate pay for quality work.

The participant was a plumbing apprentice for a commercial plumbing company and was attending Hinds Jr. College's Apprenticeship Program when he started working for himself. Since he opened his business, he has gained knowledge of how to price jobs, maintain records, and organize large jobs. Incentives, giving employees job responsibility and making them feel important by giving them praise like "great job" builds the esteem of employees and helps build trust.

This entrepreneur considered leadership development practices to include giving employees responsibility and authority, praising their work, providing on-the-job training, trusting their decisions and judgment, and taking their advice. Underpricing his first large job which caused him to lose money was his biggest business mistake.

Sharing leadership is his style of management. Taking advice from plumbing helpers is important to them and wise for him, because "two heads are always better than one when we are laying pipe fittings," he replied. From this business entrepreneur's perspective, teamwork is the best way to go.

This proprietor gets to know his customers on a first name basis, is always courteous to them, and considered customers his number one priority. He assumed it is important to pay his helpers fair wages, because their labor is needed to complete large jobs. Since their labor is valuable, he contended that it is important to show them appreciation. When discussing a job, he always says "We" instead of "I."

An insurance agent from Atlanta, Georgia, who has been in business five years started her insurance practice because she had not been given a fair chance to excel in her field by her former employer. Living by the *Golden Rule* "do onto others as you would have them do unto you," was the most important lesson she learned. This agent had basic computer skills and had obtained her insurance license when her agency was opened.

Continuing education and moral support encourages employees to grow according to this insurance agent. In addition, she contended that being supportive empowers others to reach their professional goals. Empowerment, inspiration, productivity, client retention skills, work ethics, networking education, and creative solutions are considered effective leadership strategies. Not following her instincts which led her to acquire an account with an unethical client was one of the greatest mistakes she acknowledged. This proprietor's managerial style is hands-off. Customers are treated according to the "golden rule."

A Jackson Hair Salon Manager proclaimed, "I became self-employed because I love styling hair and was good at it." He had been a hair stylist for years before he opened his salon. He had knowledge of the salon business and great communication skills before opening the shop. The most important lessons he learned was to create credit lending standards and the need to protect income with a check cashing machine.

This Salon manager said he acquired the ability to organize the salon, stock sufficient supplies, and lease space to responsible people after being a manager for 18 years. In response to the question concerning leadership strategies, he said the only employee that he manages is a cleaning lady. Customers are treated well and stylists are treated as business partners.

Active listening and limiting advice and opinions are some of the key concepts he learned over the years; he considered these concepts to be valuable in the salon business. "Most people really want someone to be supportive of the things that are going on in their lives, regardless of their life style," he contended.

Analysis of the Interviews

Some common as well as some different themes emerged from the responses. The interview responses suggested that staff development which includes on-the-job training is important to individuals as well as to a business. The literature emphasized the need to develop staff and management. Two leaders preferred a hands-on managerial style, while at least eight participants utilized a hands-off managerial style.

Only one research participant considered it important to allow subordinates to evaluate management and only one of them gave her staff the opportunity to engage in side business ventures. In spite of leadership and managerial differences among the research participants, many of the characteristics noted in the literature (compassion, goal oriented, fiscal responsible, open minded, and team oriented) of effective business leaders were corroborated by the data findings.

Fulbright (2003) said leaders should be open to new knowledge. This willingness to learn is critical given the rapid changes in technology and ways to conduct business. McCauley et al. (1998) promoted the idea that leadership development focused on building individual capacity which includes practical training programs. They further contended that training programs that provide individuals with feedback are more significant to individual growth than training that does not. They also assumed that training assessments are relevant.

Anderson (2003) reported that leaders should assess his or her skills in order to provide trainings to subordinates. Smith (2000) contended that leaders are teachers who should teach some of their own classes. Anderson says short courses (Ten Minutes of Tech, Question and Answer Sessions) may have a higher success rate than formal training sessions that last longer.

Anderson maintained that keeping a log of questions and staff learning interests such as how to scan text can lead to the creation of training sessions. Anderson noted that if training sessions include over 12 participants, it is better to have at least two instructors.

Anderson said that humor and a good rapport with adult learners go a long way. Anderson and Smith emphasized the need for leaders to provide instruction and direction to staff, whereas the program director of the television station and other respondents assumed it was important for staff to attend seminars and training sessions even if such programs were outsourced.

Vella et al. (1998) are strong supporters of the use of assessment tools. They assumed that popular education training models are effective learning techniques for adult learners. Such models offer a hands-on learning approach for training participants. They assumed that assessment should be conducted over a long-term period as opposed to the concept of assessing progress the day of the training.

The authors years of research showed that it is important to find out the expectation of training participants before they attend training programs and to assess their learning by contacting participants' months after they participate in training. This process will determine the skills and attitudes participants have applied to their jobs since participating in the training.

In addition to training, all of the small business leaders considered customer service to be very important, and they stressed the importance of treating customers and clients with great respect. One entrepreneur noted that, "customers are number one." All of the leaders suggested that customers, staff, or subordinates should be treated with respect. In fact, the term "respect" was used by most of the leaders. Maxwell (2002) maintained that respect is an important component of leadership.

Two of the male leaders suggested that a hands-on managerial approach is the best way to manage. One business owner suggested that leaders should run an operation based on their judgment and opposed sharing leadership and empowering staff with knowledge. However, the majority of the participants supported sharing leadership and following a hands-off managerial style. Likewise, the literature promoted the concept of sharing leadership and increasing individual capacity.

The U.S. Small Business Administration (2003) maintained that leaders should be team oriented. Instead of promoting an adult/child relationship with employees, leaders should create adult/adult relationships that foster team cohesiveness. Little Rock Website (2003) noted that Sam Walton (Wal-Mart Founder) said "individuals don't win, teams do." The research participant who managed a newspaper said her company supports team work.

Likewise, the plumbing business proprietor assumed that team work is the best way to go and that taking advice from plumbing helpers and partners is important. According to the Little Rock Website, one of Walton's Ten Commandments was - listen to everyone. Kouzes & Posner (2002) said leaders can foster collaboration by asking questions, listening and taking advice from subordinates. They also pointed out leaders should always say "we." This point was noted in the data by the plumbing entrepreneur, who remarked that he always said "we" instead of "I." Doty (2000) also concluded that success is about "team" and "we," not "you" and "me." In addition, Kouzes & Posner (2002) said taking advice from subordinates fosters team support.

Fulbright (2003) maintained that a business owner's ability to set goals and plans for success are skills required to succeed. Failing to engage in long-range planning and not creating a cash reserve were some of the biggest mistakes that a real estate investor admitted. The program director of the television program said her strengths included the ability to set goals and be objective oriented. The data and literature emphasize that setting goals and engaging in long-term planning are important leadership traits. Fulbright (2003) contended that "Intense goal orientation is the characteristic of every successful entrepreneurs" (p. 2).

Most of the lessons that research participants learned through experience related to fiscal management such as preparing taxes and sufficient bid proposals, establishing business reserves, investing in the stock market, and maintaining books. As Kouzes and Posner (2002) alleged, an effective leadership component includes guiding the growth and prosperity of companies which include managing resources appropriately.

The U.S. Small Business Administration said today's leaders are visionaries, who are both learners and teachers. Smith (2000) also alleged that leaders are teachers. Furthermore, Smith emphasized that leaders should teach some of their own classes. Fulbright (2003) said a study showed that being open to learning was an aspect of a successful entrepreneur. The pest control owner noted that he learned to be open-minded. The cleaning service research participant says business owners are always learning. The plumber business proprietor reported that he takes advice from employees. One of the insurance agents said engaging in continuing education contributes to staff development.

Kouzes & Posner (2002) pointed out that stories teach values and are good learning models. For example, Abraham Lincoln loved *Aesop's Fables, Pilgrim's Progress,* Shakespeare's plays, and the King James Bible. Martin Luther King Jr. was a student of the U.S. Constitution, a seminarian, and a student of the world's great philosophers. The literature and data suggested that effective leaders are learners and teachers.

Wendy's International, Inc. Website (2003) said one of the values that Dave Thomas lived by was giving back. He felt that supporting children who were waiting to be adopted was an important charitable cause for him because he had been adopted himself and understood the significance of having a stable family life.

The newspaper partner said the need to give back to the community was one of the greatest lessons she learned during her many years of business experience. Williams (2004) reported that 91% of small businesses support local charities and groups and these businesses contribute millions of dollars each year to their communities.

The responses and the literature suggested that giving back to the community is an important value and quality of a business leader while networking is a business strategy. Fulbright (2003) stressed the need for leaders to constantly look for ways to network. Forming partnerships with people who can support one's business is valuable. To be successful leaders should have good networking skills. One of the insurance agents' alleged staff should be taught how to network, and the newspaper partner said one of the lessons she learned over the years was the importance of networking.

Kouzes & Posner (2002) reported that it is important for leaders and associates to be connected to networks. They also alleged that associates should be connected to each other. Brain power is essential to succeed in the new economy. Making something happen is a function of what we know and who we know.

Fulbright (2003) maintained that a study showed that successful entrepreneurs share various characteristics like working hard. She added that some of them put in 15 to 18 hours per day because they love what they do. The cleaning service owner said she learned several important lessons including the fact that a business owner had to work hard, always watch out for pit falls, and work long hours. The cleaning service entrepreneur has managed to surpass the 20 year business mark.

Ray Kroc made a lot of sacrifices after becoming a partner with Dick and Maurice McDonald in 1955. Kroc worked long hours even though he was in his mid-fifties and he withheld his salary for eight years. Between 1955 and 1959, Kroc succeeded in opening 100 restaurants and in 1961 Kroc purchased the exclusive rights to McDonald's from the brothers for $2.7 million. By 1963, there were 500 restaurants.

Three of the entrepreneurs considered pay increases and raises as a single means of encouraging and enhancing employee growth. The other research participants suggest that pay increases, moral support, work independence, praise, training, and other concepts coupled together enhance and encourage subordinates and staff to grow.

Kouzes & Posner (2003) reported that contrary to the belief of many managers a study conducted in 1949 showed that employees placed more value on being appreciated, listened to, and being informed of what was going on in the company than they did on pay, job security, and advancement opportunities. The data and literature alike also pointed out that employees are human beings, who need to feel that they matter.

One Manager had an open-door policy that gave employees the opportunity to offer suggestions and to critique management. Smith (2000) stated that management should give employees permission to disagree with management. I found this to be an interesting point which is an idea that I suggested when I was a program manager. However, the idea was discarded by other managers, and it was never implemented.

The importance of allowing staff to evaluate their superiors was supported by the literature. McCauley et al. (1998) suggested that it is a good idea to have the performance of managers assessed. Kouzes & Posner (2003) said leaders should be evaluated by subordinates to assess how well they are encouraging others. The program director of a television station stated that regular evaluations are important to employees because people need to understand how they are doing professionally.

Furthermore, only one business (the newspaper) manager reported that she allowed staff to earn extra income through company clientele like preparing résumés and graphic design projects. This concept was supported in the literature. Buchanan (2001) says one-to-one management includes funding for staff engineers and scientists to deliver their non-work related research at far-flung professional conferences.

Buchanan (2001) noted that John Metzger, who manages a staff of 30 plus, has an extraordinary award system. Metzger's staff receive $500 of reimbursements for physical fitness (gym memberships, a bicycle), $600 for relaxation (guitar lessons, vacations), and $1000 for education. Metzger says "We're open to individuals telling us whatever they need to be balanced in their lives. We want people to be passionate about life, hobbies, and outside pursuits because we want passionate people" (p. 6). After implementing a Management One-to-One Program, the company's turnover dropped from 15 to two percent. Metzger supported non-work related ideas of employees and individualizes his award program.

Kouzes & Posner (2003) recommended that if companies consistently utilized the same award and recognition programs from one year to the next, they might want to allow staff to assess the programs. Based on the findings in this study, my personal experience, and feedback from other co-workers, a bi-yearly routine award ceremony becomes old over time and individualizing awards would be appreciated more by employees.

Smith (2000) suggested that managers should offer awards to individuals for reasons other than "Best Employee of the Month/Year," etc. Smith emphasized the importance of having frequent, informal recognition/award celebrations for employees.

The director of the television station said rewarding and recognizing staff contributions is important. The plumbing business owner recalled that employees like to receive praise and that leaders should show staff that they are appreciated. He emphasized the significance of saying "thank you and great job." Last year, the newspaper business rewarded their staff by taking them and their family on a trip to Disney World.

The interviewees addressed the significance of the leaders and subordinates relationship which is a central theme in the literature. Isidro (2001) noted that an entrepreneur's key to client relationships is understanding client expectation. He said service business managers should ask clients how they want services completed. *The Women Today Magazine* (2004) advised that effective leaders should be visible to members of their organizations by visiting with them. The interview data suggested that leaders should follow the golden rule and show admiration and respect for staff and clients/customers.

Taylor (2004) maintained that managers can retain good employees by developing ways to give staff responsibility, the freedom to act, and the ability to feel good about themselves. One of the insurance agents considered employees learning client retention skills as an effective leadership strategy. The plumber entrepreneur assumed that giving employees job responsibility helps build trust and the esteem of employees. The television station manager proclaimed that an effective leadership strategy is maintaining an atmosphere in which staff can make decisions without fear of error. This strategy connects to Taylor's "freedom to act" concept.

Kouzes & Posner (2002) identified listening to constituents and taking their advice as a means of strengthening leaders ability to appreciate the purpose of others. The authors added that "listening is one of the key characteristics of exemplary leaders" (p. 187). Furthermore, Kouzes & Posner said listening demonstrates leaders' respect for others and their ideas and Anderson (2003) emphasized that effective leaders are good listeners.

The car rental salesman said his listening skills and knowledge of fishing were his strengths for his bait sales enterprise. These skills helped him select the appropriate bait to sell to fisherman. Active listening was one of the key concepts that the salon owner learned during his years of experience. The real estate investor said she learned how to listen to the tenants' side of the story when problems arose because people appreciated being treated respectfully.

The interview data and literature findings suggested in general that employee incentives, customer service, planning and setting goals, team work, open mindedness, hard work, building trust, and individual and organizational capacity building are important aspects of leadership processes.

Lessons from Small Business Leaders

The 12 business leaders, who participated in this study, were all asked "What are the most important lessons you learned as a small business leader? Their responses are below.

Industry	**Experience**	**Lesson**
Maid Service	20 Years	Small business owners have to work hard and long hours. They have to work out the pit falls, and they are always learning.
Insurance	5 Years	Live by the *golden rule;* do unto others, as you would have them do unto you.
Pest Control	9 Years	I've learned how to deal with people and how to be open minded.
Newspaper	24 Years	I've learned that you have to give back to the community. I also learned to accept my business role and the importance of networking.
Real Estate	27 Years	I learned to treat others as you want to be treated, to be honest, and that dishonesty does not go far.
Multiple Business Ventures	60 Years	He learned from his father that a person has to know more than anyone else knows in his line of work.
Insurance	10 Years	Learned to believe in God and the importance of accepting constructive criticism.
Property Rental	20 Years	I learned the importance of having a financial reserve for major repairs.
Television Production	10 Years	I learned to pay attention to details and to select key personnel and partners wisely.

Plumbing	5 Years	I learned to maintain a reserve for business expenses.
Salon Owner	20 Years	I learned to create credit standards and the importance of a check cashing machine.
Sales	30 Years	I learned that products sell themselves and good communication sells you-the sales person.

The lessons above are examples of what the small business owners and managers have learned since they have been in their leadership positions. For example, a trait of an effective leader is following the golden rule and accepting constructive criticism. Good business practices include creating expense reserves and networking with those who can share resources.

Based on the findings in this study, the above "lessons" are characteristics of effective leaders and are models of good business practices.

IV. DISCUSSION & IMPLICATIONS

As one of the interviewees stated small businesses are the pulse of the economy, and small business leaders should be effective in order to achieve business success. In addition, this study *Characteristics and business strategies of successful small business leaders* offers a number of suggestions that others can follow.

The literature supported the data that was collected through the interviews. The practice that flexible work schedules are good employee incentives from the interviews was supported by the literature. As two of the interviewees stated, people appreciate flexible hours, which allow them to accompany their children, spouse, or family members to a doctor's appointment. Likewise, Buchanan (2001) stated that "Hours as flexible as a Romanian gymnast," is a creative award. The data suggested an underlining theme that employees, customers, and subordinates be treated with the utmost respect.

Kouzes & Posner (2002) promoted five leadership practices including modeling the way, inspiring a shared vision, challenging the process, enabling others to act, and encouraging the heart. Several interviewees say leaders should model the way. The interview data suggested that people should be challenged, allowed to make decisions, and encouraged. However, the interviews did not corroborate the authors' point to inspire a shared vision among subordinates.

Recommendations

Effective leaders have common characteristics and utilize various business strategies. Leaders should strive to become experts in their chosen fields, respect staff and customers, provide on-the-job-training to subordinates, and utilize effective networking systems among other things. In addition leaders can adhere to the following principles:

1. Engage in constant educational activities to increase individual capacity in one's field.
2. Follow the golden rule, "Do onto others as one would want others to do unto him or her."
3. Understand how to maintain books and other fiscal matters before starting a business.
4. Give back and support community causes.
5. Seek advice from subordinates, peers, and other leaders.
6. Be open-minded and willing to learn new ideas.
7. Learn the most common reasons that businesses fail.
8. Obtain technical support from the Small Business Administration and other business support programs during planning stages.
9. Develop regular assessments to evaluate the performance of staff and leadership.
10. Develop great relationships with subordinates.
11. Provide incentives that individuals would appreciate as opposed to carrying out systematic award programs.
12. Offer frequent and informal recognition/award celebrations for employees.
13. Leaders should evaluate the performance of subordinates and be willing to receive feedback and criticism from others.
14. Managers should be willing to create adult/adult relationships with staff and create work adhesion.
15. Take a hard look at organizational culture and tradition and discard traditions that do not make sense today.
16. Operate competitive enterprises and develop good networking skills.

17. Be aware of current business market trends, pricing standards, and service fees and rates.
18. Admit mistakes because subordinates will cover up their own errors if leaders hide their mistakes.
19. Be cautious of public criticism which can embarrass and alienate staff.
20. Leaders should emphasize the strengths and contributions of others instead of building their own egos, and
21. Leaders should be humble, have empathy, and be willing to see things from the perspective of others.

In addition to the above recommendations, business leaders may utilize the information from the *Business Resources* table that was abstracted from the Small Business Administration. These organizations offer small business resources and technical assistance (Williams 2004). The business resource guide is provided herein.

APPENDICES

Interview questions

1. Why did you decide to become self-employed or assume your leadership role?

2. What are the most important lessons you learned as a small business leader?

3. What skills did you have when you opened your small business or assumed your leadership position?

4. What skills did you acquire after you established your business or after assuming your position?

5. What are your assumptions concerning what enhances and encourages employees to grow?

6. State five effective leadership strategies?

7. What are some of the most memorable business mistakes you have made?

8. What is your managerial style?

9. How do you treat staff and customers/clients?

Meredith C. McGee
Address
Jackson, MS
Phone Fax E-mail

October 7, 2003

Participant
Address
City, State Zip

Dear Participant:

Subject: Research Participation **Consent Letter**

Consent Letter

I am a graduate student majoring in Rural Community Development & Public Policy at Antioch University McGregor which is located in Yellow Springs, OH. I understand that you have operated and managed a real estate investment venture for several decades. Because of your expertise on small business success, I am inviting you to participate in a research study that I am conducting on the impact of effective leadership development on small business success.

This study will compile the raw data collected from interviews and compare it with popular literature on leadership development including managerial styles, incentive programs, assessment tools, training, and other areas of leadership that effect business success. I will be conducting interviews (30 minute minimum) with small business leaders and owners who reside in the South and who have owned or lead a small business for at least five years.

The confidentiality all participants will be maintained and this study will adhere to the code of ethics required by Antioch University McGregor and its governing bodies. A consent form is attached. Please complete the form. Your signature will denote your intent to participate. Thank you in advance for your cooperation.

Sincerely yours,

Meredith C. McGee

Enclosure: Consent Form

CONSENT FORM

I am interested in participating in the leadership development study being conducted by Meredith C. McGee, a research student at Antioch University McGregor. Yes or No

October 19 - 25, 2003, is a good week for me to set up an appointment. Yes or No

October 26 - 30, 2003, is a good week for me to set up an appointment. Yes or No

Best time and date for interview:
____ Lunch during the week of October __________.
____ Lunch on the weekend of October __________.

I am available on __________________ (date).
I prefer a *person to person* interview. Yes or No
I prefer a *phone* interview. Yes or No
I consent to have my photograph included in this study. Yes or No
I consent to have an area of my business photographed.
Yes or No
You may fax this form to 601… mail it to the address on the letterhead, or I will be happy to pick the form up.

Thank you for your time and consideration.

Business Resources

Assn of Small Business Development Centers
www.asbdc-us.org
(703) 764-9850
Businesslaw.gov

www.businesslaw.gov

FIRSTGOV.GOV

www.firstgov.gov/Business/Business_Gateway.shtml

FTC

www.ftc.gov/ftc/businessinfo/consumer.htm

The U.S. Junior Chamber (JAYCEES)

www.usjaycees.org

(800) 529-2337

National Association for the Self-Employed

www.nase.org

(800) 232-6273

The National Black Chamber of Commerce Inc.

www.nationalbcc.org

(202) 466-6888

National Business Association
www.nationalbusiness.org
(800) 456-0400
SBA

www.sba.gov

www.sba.gov/training

Service Corps of Retired Executives (SCORE)
www.score.org

(800) 634-0245

Small Business Advancement National Center
www.sbaer.uca.edu

United States Hispanic Chamber of Commerce
www.ushcc.com

(202) 842-1212

U.S. Business Advisor

www.business.gov

U.S. Pan Asian-American Chamber of Commerce
www.uspaacc.com

(202) 296-5221

(William, 2004, p. 43)

REFERENCES

Anderson, M. A. (2003). Jump-starting staff development. *School Library Journal, 49(8), 36-38.*

Buchanan, L. (2001, Oct.). Managing one-to-one. *Inc.com,* 1-6. Retrieved October 7, 2003, from http://www.pf.inc.com/magazine/20011001/23479.html

Doty, C. S. (2000). Humility as a leadership attribute. *Military Review*, 80(5), 89 - 90.

Emmott, B. (Ed) (2004, April 24). Less glamour, more profit. *The Economist* 371(8372), p. 11.

Edmond Jr., A. A. (2004, May). Make-or-break leadership lessons from the apprentice, 34(10), pp. 108-114.

Fulbright, J. (2003). 10 Secrets of successful entrepreneurs. *PowerHomeBiz.com,* 19, 1 - 4. Retrieved March 12, 2004, from http://www.powerhomebiz.com/vol19secrets.htm.

Headd, B. (2000). The Characteristics of small-business employers. [Electronic version]. *Monthly Labor Review, 13 – 18.* Retrieved August 18, 2003, from http://www.sba.vog/advo/stats/.

Hoffman, T. (2004). Grooming tomorrow's leaders. *Computerworld,* 38, 36.

Isidro, I.M. (2001). 10 Tips for a successful service business. *PowerHomeBiz.com*, 57, 1 - 4. Retrieved December 1, 2003, from http://www.powerhomebiz.com/vol57/service.htm

Jamison, K. (1984). *The Nibble theory and the kernel of power*. Mahwah, NJ: Paulist Press.

Kouzes, J. M., & Posner, B. Z. (2003). *Encouraging the heart: a leader's guide to rewarding and recognizing subordinates.* San Francisco, CA: Jossey-Bass Publishing.

Kouzes, J. M., & Posner, B. Z. (2002).*The Leadership challenge.* San Francisco, CA: Jossey-Bass Publishing Co.

Lauer, C. S. (2002, February 25). The Basic recipe for a leader. *Modern Healthcare*, 32, 33.

Little Rock, AR Website (2004). *Sam Walton retail success story.* Retrieved March 25, 2004, from http://littlerock.about.com/cs/homeliving/a/aasamwaton_p.htm

Maxwell, J. C. (2002). *Leadership 101: what every leader needs to know.* Nashville, TN: Thomas Nelson Publishing.

McCauley, C. D., Moxley, R. S., & Velsor, E. V. (Eds.). (1998). The *Center for creative leadership handbook of leadership development.* San Francisco, CA: Jossey-Bass.

McDonald's Corporation Website (2004). *About McDonald's.* Retrieved March 28, 2004 from, http://www.mcdonalds.com/corp.html/

Power Home Biz.com (2001). *10 Tips for a successful service business.* Retrieved December 1, 2003, from http://www.powerhomebiz.comvol57/service.htm

Rodriguez, G. (2003). Three indicators of a successful business. *PowerHomeBiz.com, 15, 1 – 2.* Retrieved March 12, 2003, from http://www.powerhome.biz.com/vol15/3indicators.htm

Smith, G. P. (2000, April 3). Good leaders set the pace, Encourage Employees to Excel. *New Orleans City Business,* 20(41), p. 24.

Taylor, C. R. (2004, March). Retention leadership. *T+D,* 58(3), 40-46.

U.S. Small Business Administration. (2002). *SBA: Leadership traits.* Retrieved October 7, 2003 from http://www.sba.gov/managing/leadership/traits.html

U.S. Small Business Administration. (2002). *SBA: Small business week 2002 winners.* Retrieved November 19, 2003, from http://appl.sba.gov.sbsuccess/2002dsp_winner_info.cfm?Bus_ID=25

U.S. Small Business Administration. (2003, June). Small business economic indicators for 2002. Retrieved August 18, 2003, from http://www.sba.govladvol.

Vella, J., Berardinelli, P., and Burrow, J. (1997). *How do they know they know: evaluating adult learning.* San Francisco, CA: Jossey-Bass Publishers.

Wendy's International, Inc. (2003). *Dave Thomas, father, founder, friend 1932-2002*. Retrieved March 26, 2004 from, http://www.wendy's.com/w-1-0.shtml

Wijewardena, H., Zoysa, A. D., Fonseka, T., & Perera, B. (2004). The Impact of planning and control sophistication on performance of small and medium-sized enterprises: evidence from Sri Lanka, *Journal of Small Business Management,* 42(2), 203-217.

Williams, G. (2004, March). It's a small world after all. *Entrepreneur, 32(5),* 39-43.

Women Today Magazine (2004). *The 7 Traits of leaders: how many do you share?* Retrieved March 12, 2004 from, http://www.womentodaymagazine.com/career/7leader.html

Zeuli, K. & O'Shea, K. (2017). Small business growth. *Economic Development Journal*, 16(1), 15-21.

ACKNOWLEDGEMENTS

Many thanks to my younger sister, Willa Coleman Ridgeway (Reya Peach) for writing the prelude, and her youngest child, Calla Ridgeway who shared a special poem she wrote to our mother. Much love to Billie Jean Young, the author of *Fear Not the Fall, Now! How Do You*?, and *Family Secrets*, who encouraged me to write poetry a decade ago, and my aunt Chappell Meredith, a retired educator who believed my poetry was worthy of publication after hearing me read *Lynch Street* at a family reunion banquet.

I sincerely thank my parents, fore-parents, former supervisors, teachers, and leaders: James H. Meredith, Arthur C. Meredith, Everett H. Meredith, Hon. John L. Allbritton, Frederick J. Gant, Esq., Socrates Garrett, Minnie Garrett, Alice Thomas-Tisdale, the late Alvin Binder, Esq., Bob Owens, Esq., Hon. Denise Sweet Owens, Melbah M. Smith, Ben Burkett, Ralph Paige, Shirley Sherrod, Alice Paris, John Zippert, Starry Krueger, CJ Jones, Lee Harper, Alexis Spencer-Byers, Phillip K. Reed, D.L. and Helen Govan, Hollis Watkins, Mike Sayer, Ophelia Kelley, Brenda Hyde, … and Dorothy Stewart whose guidance anchored the bright lights comprising the building blocks which is slowly leading the way up the stairs out of the pits of economic darkness.

AUTHOR'S NOTE

Odyssey offers 42 entertaining and inspiring poems. There are three chapters of poems: **Chapter 1** *Something Chronicled,* **Chapter 2** *Something Inspiring,* **Chapter 3** *Something Blue. The lethal game* of chance discourages youth from playing the deadly game of Russian Roulette. *Little Susie Q* glorifies sexual abstinence, *The Bookstore* describes racial profiling, and *Lynch Street* is based on actual historical facts about Reconstruction leader John Roy Lynch (1847-1939).

Chapter 4 *Something Spoken* includes several speeches by the author. **Chapter 5** *Something Written* contains articles on topics ranging from consumer issues to the basics of forming a business. **Chapter 6** *Something Studied* compared the leadership strategies of 12 small business leaders in the south with Sam Walton, who founded Walmart, Dave Thomas, the forefather of Wendy's International, and Ray Kroc who transformed McDonalds from a regional based restaurant chain into a global giant.

ABOUT THE AUTHOR

Meredith Coleman McGee is the author of *Nashida: Visits the Mississippi State Capitol*, *Nashida: Visits the Smith Robertson Museum*, *James Meredith: Warrior and the America that created him* and co-author of *Married to Sin*. Her poetry is published in the anthologies: *Virtues from the heart* and *Timeless Voices*. She is the lead author of *My First Book Series* (six volume pre-school primer set).

McGee resides in Jackson, Mississippi where she is a professional writer for Typing Solutions Résumé & Etc typingsolutions.biz the acquisition editor/publisher of Meredith Etc, a small press meredithetc.com, the blog administrator of shopheirs.com, and a contributing writer for the Jackson Advocate, a weekly newspaper jacksonadvocateonline.com/.

McGee is a rural fellow with the Rural Leadership Development Network; she is a member of the Sankofa Reading Group and the Learning Tree Book Club; she is associated with the Clinton Ink-Slingers, and Women for Progress; she founded Heirs United Investment Club in 1997, a Booker T. Washington Economic Summit award recipient. McGee was previously the acquisition editor of Mose Dantzler Press mosedpress.com, owned a convenience store, Sunrise Foods # II (TS & M Super Stop), was a business developer for Mississippi Association of Cooperatives, was assistant director of development for Voice of Calvary Ministries, and was a community organizer for Southern Echo.

Meredith Coleman McGee's blog page
https://meredithetc.com/meredith-coleman-mcgee/

INDEX

Meredith Etc Book Titles:

Odyssey
Nashida: Visits the Smith Robertson Museum
Nashida: Visits the Mississippi State Capitol
By Meredith Coleman McGee

Reverse Guilty Plea by
The New Populist Party
William Trest, Jr.

Starkishia: Estrella by Starkishia

Southern Jewel: The Elements Within by Ty A Patterson

Woman Preach
Social Justice and Christianity
By Rev. Dr. Louis Blake Hathorn

Saving the Manatees
By JaNiya Williams; illustrated by Calla Ridgeway

Death by Association Vol. 1 *Retaliation* Vol. 2 *Deception*
By Anthony Ellis

Mary's Story & Song
By Mary Haralson Coleman with Starkishia

My Brother Bo: Addicted in Paradise
By Richard Hulse

Tragedy, Yet, Triumphant
By Loretha Wallace and Loretta Wallace Ellis

The Southern Phoenix
Juvenile Offenders: From Big Wheels to the Big House
By Rosemary Jenkins

My First Book Series
Meredith Coleman McGee, Hazel Hall, et al.

NOTES

Chapter One

[i]Cellie is a prisoner's cell mate.

Chapter Four

[ii] Kathy Sykes (Mississippi State Representative 2016-) is the woman challenging Charlotte Reeves in the article, *Last Two Miles of Meredith's Walk for the Poor*.

[iii] Mr. Meredith's reference to General Hampton refers to General Samuel Chapman Armstrong who headed the Hampton Institution (located in the countryside of Virginia) where Booker T. Washington was educated. Washington founded Tuskegee Institute from the Hampton school model.

[iv] Judy Alsobrooks is the wife of Civil Rights icon James H. Meredith. She used her maiden name on air.

www.ingramcontent.com/pod-product-compliance
Lightning Source LLC
Chambersburg PA
CBHW030357310726
48979CB00001B/341
* 9 7 8 0 9 9 9 3 2 2 6 3 5 *